TROGS AFLOAT

TROGS AFLOAT

BY CHARLES GARDNER

Published by

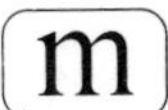

MIDAS BOOKS

12 Dene Way, Speldhurst, Tunbridge Wells, Kent.

Also in the series:
The Great Trog Conspiracy by Charles Gardner, OBE
Trogs in the Suburbs by Bill Lampitt

ISBN 0 85936 028 8

PRICE £1.00

Drawings by Mike Mehra
Printed in England by Errey's Printers, Heathfield, Sussex.

Introduction

As a result of generations of propaganda plus an actual supporting fact or two like the Armada, the Golden Hind, Aboukir Bay, Copenhagen, Trafalgar, the Graf Spee and Compass Rose, the Island Race properly regards anything that floats on water as being part of its National Heritage. Furthermore, the only British thing then to do with such a floating device is either to cause it to be propelled further or faster than anyone else's floating device or, failing that, to lay it close alongside until the enemy strikes, sinks, runs aground, or shouts "starboard"!

I have already observed and reported on the warlike instincts which are liberated as soon as the landborne British get behind the wheel of a car. On the road this instinct, as I have revealed, is organised and disciplined by the Great Trog Movement and controlled by the dreaded TROGPU, so that each Trog knows and keeps his place in the battle order. Trog actions on the roads are fought by massed Trog troops, trained to the ounce, and who are the masters of a few simple basic and effective tactics which, even though well understood, are still difficult to defeat. *(See "The Great Trog Conspiracy".)* In military terms, Trogs A'wheel fight set piece infantry battles on ground of their own choosing. They use tactics akin to the British Squares and Wellington or Lord Haigh would be proud of them.

But Trogs Afloat are another story. It is on board and in command of some kind of boat that each liberated Trog becomes, at last, his own Walter Mitty man. He is Nelson, he is Drake, Bligh, Chichester, Rose, Knox Johnston, Blyth, James Onedin and Hornblower. He is a white scarved Captain D – "Port Ten – Make Smoke" – he is Errol Flyn, Johnny Mills, and, above all, he is Jack Hawkins. The navy's here and steer for the sound of the guns!

Put a Trog in a motor car and he will dutifully and meekly combine with all other Trogs to form impassable 30 mph crocodiles from end to end of the A27. But put him in a Mirror dinghy and, in a snap of his braces, he is transformed into a single-ship action man, a lone wolf of the sea, seeing no signals and calling for the Master Gunner.

So, on every pond and boating lake, on every gravel pit and river and broad and in every estuary and harbour, the Island Race, at summer week-ends, sprouts a hundred thousand bold sea raiders – each planning to cut out the enemy against dreadful odds and to return, treasure laden, to Glenda Jackson, to be nudged in the ribs and called 'Her Old Sea Dog'.

It is at the local boating lake that the Troglings first taste the sweetness of individual command. There, at happy play, they crash and collide, jam each other into corners, and belt each other about the ears with the oars. Only too soon will they graduate into hire cruisers on the Thames and the Broads, into assorted dinghies everywhere, and into motorised skimming dishes being rescued in sea sagas off Southend.

So it is in humble tribute to the indomitable spirit of the Trogs Afloat and of the brave crews of Trog Mums who go with them, that I dedicate this book. In it I seek to capture some of their moments of glory and, meanwhile, I beg you, dear reader, to reflect that while they are afloat they cannot also be on the roads.

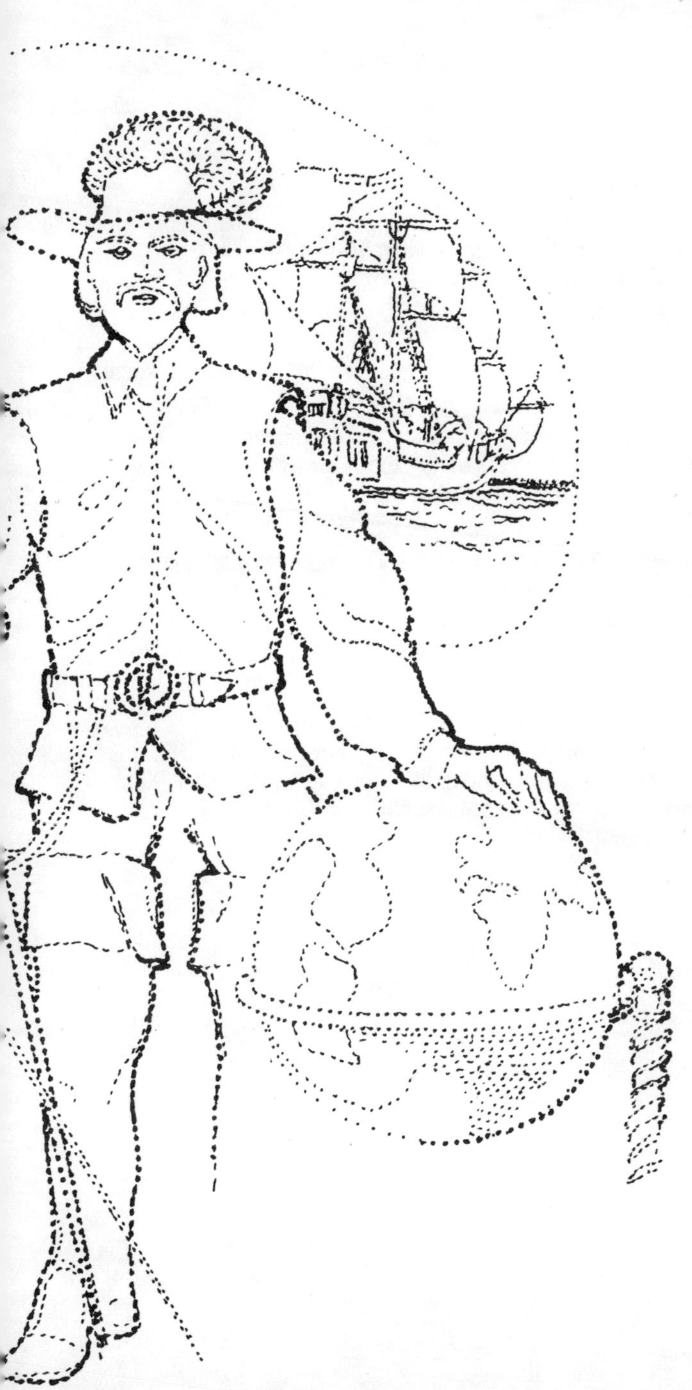

THE AUTHOR

Charles Gardner O.B.E., A.F.R.Ae.S.

.... is still remembered for his "Battle of Britain" BBC broadcast from Dover Cliffs. He was BBC Air Correspondent for many years, both before and after the war and he and Richard Dimbleby were the first two BBC Home News Staff reporters and, later, in 1939/40, the first two BBC War Correspondents sent to France.

After the Battle of Britain, Gardner became an R.A.F. pilot himself and flew Coastal Command Catalinas in the Atlantic, Mediterranean and Far East Theatres before joining the staff of the then Lord Louis Mountbatten on the latter's appointment as Supreme Allied Commander South East Asia.

Mr. Gardner left the BBC staff in 1953 to join Sir George Edwards' team at Weybridge as a Senior Executive in the Aircraft Industry and he has been Publicity Manager of the British Aircraft Corporation since its formation in 1960. He has given the commentary on the Farnborough Air Show for many years and is the author of a number of aviation books.

Mr. Gardner is married, lives near Leatherhead, has two sons, a daughter and four grandchildren - all of whom are expert Trog Spotters. He used to play a lot of cricket but now concentrates on sailing and golf and is proud of being an Associate of the Inner Magic Circle.

1

To say nothing of the dog.

As we begin our studies it is proper to emphasise that Troggery – whether a'wheel or afloat – has little to do with class or cash. Some of the more noteworthy shore-based Trog Actions of all time have been initiated by Rolls-Royces and Bentleys. Similarly, just as many outstanding deeds of Troggery afloat have been accomplished by gin palaces which have cost a good 50 grand (cocktail lounge extra). Conversely, some of the most non-Trog of sailors boast only a second-hand Wayfarer dinghy, or a ten year old Enterprise.

The Trogs, then, afloat as a'wheel, are a classless society, and this is readily observable by any student who cares to start his Trog Recognition course at the most readily available of all Trog spotting areas – the Thames Valley. And what is true of the Thames is, I doubt not, equally true of the Severn, the Trent, the Greater or Lesser Ouse, to say nothing of the Welland, the Nene, the Conway, the Dart and all those other Rolls-Royce aero engines.

My own observations have shown that there are five main kinds of private boat to be seen on the Thames.

- Rowboats (as in J K Jerome – with or without outboard motor).
- Canoes.
- Privately owned cruisers.
- Hire cruisers.
- Sailing dinghies.

Sailing Dinghies

These mainly belong to members of one of the sailing clubs whose bases are huts or converted river-bank dwellings hidden behind a forest of masts, often at a river bend. There seems to be one sailing club for about every mile of the Thames and, in the main, the members are non-Trog. They also tend to be more aggressively nautical in speech and dress than their counterparts on the coast and, truth to tell, they are every bit as skilful – maybe more so. River dinghy sailors are mainly there for the racing as well as the beer, and racing on the river is unrewarding work. In the first place one

bank or the other gets in the way about every hundred yards involving a simple choice between going about or going aground. And if ever the wind is nicely on the beam on one bit of the course you will have it on the nose round the next bend – and the next bend is seldom far away. Trees, banks, buildings and bridges screen the breeze, whirl it about, or leave flat calms, and although there isn't a tide, there is still a downstream current – dwindling at the edges and strong in the middle. There are also 14 ft fishing rods and lines, waved in rows from each bank like an archway of swords of honour at a wedding, plus non-stop processions of other river traffic, including pleasure steamers which fill the Thames like the Q.E. fills the narrower bits of Southampton water. The "ditch crawlers", as sea-sailors call them, may well be mad, but Trogs they are not.

The one thing they all need to have to survive is a good shouting voice. On an average day you can hear a Thames dinghy race for upwards of a mile. With six Merlin Rockets, or GP.14's, or Cadets, or what not, line abreast, all heading for the same bank. and with twelve people shouting for water as three cruisers, a tug and ten fishing lines come at them, the result, in effective perceived noise decibels, can be heard at Staines above the ambient from London Airport. I also doubt if there is ever a legal winner of a Thames dinghy race. By the time there have been two giant bank-to-bank tacks you have a situation that the lead boats are zigging on the starboard tack (ie. with the wind coming from their starboard or right-hand side) and the others are still zagging on port (wind the other way). As starboard boats have a right of way over port boats – and both are now mingled in the wash of a passing cruiser – there soon isn't a competitor left in the race who isn't flying a protest flag (off-white handkerchief). Some Thames sailors wrap the protest motif on before they start and have a quick release cord. This they pull the first time they yell "starboard" to claim a right of way which they haven't a hope of getting.

For a simple Sunday morning's fun take station near the windward turning marker of any Thames dinghy race, stuff your ears with cotton wool and wait for it. There are those who say that a helmsman who can win consistently on the Thames can win anywhere. I doubt that very much. Consistent victory on the Thames must owe at least as much to the helmsman's team of lawyers and witnesses and to his lung power as to his skill. If, however, you are still tempted to have a bash – and bash is about the right word – don't let me stop you.

It is also possible (just) to sail a dinghy on the river for pleasure in a non-competitive way. But for heaven's sake sail it upstream, however tempting the down-stream wind conditions of the moment may be. It can be a long long paddle back against the stream (always carry paddles) for, unlike at sea, there isn't any chance at all that the stream is going to "turn". At least not above Teddington it isn't. There are, I know, those who produce a furtive small outboard for the upstream journey home, but to put an outboard on a sailing dinghy is TROG POSITIVE PLUS. It is preferable to go ashore and catch a bus to fetch your car and trailer, or even to cadge a tow. Anything, in fact, rather than mount an engine. The truth is that *"Nelson never had an engine"* and if you ever want to be fully accepted afloat as a non-Trog sailor then that is sentence number one to write in your notebook. Many other of the "memorable sentences" which the non-Trog must learn and obey also start with the words, *"Nelson never had....."*. You will, in your sailing life, encounter this extreme philosophy in many forms and as good an ad hoc answer as I have been able to think of is, "Yes, but Nelson had a crew of eight hundred". Nonetheless, an outboard engine on a class sailing dinghy is Trog by any standards – Nelson's or other.

Canoes

These are non-Trog too. They are propelled relentlessly by earnest adventurers seeking a Duke of Edinburgh award or some such, in the teeth of weirs and waterfalls. They sit for hours in the roughest of the broken water, doing slow rolls and other acrobatic tricks and occasionally get on the telly on a poor afternoon on Grandstand. They tend to wear jungle hats and tropical battledress and are covered with proficiency badges. Admire them and move on. They are doing no harm to anyone and, who knows, they may even be enjoying themselves.

Private Cruisers

These provide the most rewarding field for the riverside Trog-spotter. There are thousands of cruisers on the Thames and the overwhelming majority of them are as Trog as all get out. The testing place to observe them is on the approaches to – in – and on the departure from – a lock.

On all inland water ways it is the locks which sort 'em out. To help you understand this it should be explained that water flows downhill, and has so seldom been observed to flow un-aided in the opposite direction that you may take it as an axiom that it doesn't. The original untouched-by-human-hand rivers of the world come downhill – mostly to the sea – in a series of

tumbles, rapids, waterfalls and weirs. These are splendid only for the canoeists (who regard locks as sissy and as things which Big Chief Broken Water never had). At this point I observe that when the "rapids" are too tough, or shooting them is, by law, illegal, the canoeists can carry their craft along the bank. The captain of a river cruiser cannot do this, so locks there always are. They by-pass the waterfalls and provide a simple means of transition by lift from the natural water level below the falls to the higher natural water level above them – or vice versa.

You can, therefore, either lock "up" (ie. to higher things up stream) or "down" – and the same lock – being, as it were, a two-way valve – caters for both traffic streams – though not at the same time.

When "locking up" you enter at the lower level through the open lock gates (large and more or less water tight doors) to face the upstream gates which are already shut. Your boat is then afloat in an "empty" lock and the bare walls on either side tower nakedly and slimily prison-like, skywards. The downstream gates close behind you, and you are in a walled coffin, hanging onto chains, ladder-rungs or rings which are set into the wall at intervals, boats for the tying-to.

The upstream gates – or rather the lower sliding panels of them – are now cautiously raised open and water rushes in from the higher level. The lock fills and your boat – you hope – rises with the water until you emerge into the daylight about level with the quay-side. The upstream gates now swing out to open wide, and off you go towards the next lock which is seldom more than a couple of miles away and probably only a mile, where all is to do again.

The use of each lock will, on the Thames, be paid for in your boat licence, at which the lock-keeper will always take a quick gander as you come through. If you haven't got one prominently displayed, as is required, then you are arrested, put in chains, taken to a prison hulk somewhere off Gravesend and are never heard of again.

The scope for Troggery – accidental or malicious – in and around each and every lock – whether going up or down – is infinite.

In the first place, you can assume that all locks will, as you approach them, be on the point of slamming the gates shut in your face. This is a law of nature and a bye-law of the Thames Conservancy Board, who are 'God' on the Thames above Teddington. As the gates snap-to, half a cable from your bows, you know you now have to wait for the lock to fill with water, for its elevated contents to chug on out, for the new occupants to crowd in and for the whole cycle to be repeated as a lock-load is duly locked down to your level. Then, when the "down" boats have duly gone their sneering ways – you can finally go in and be translated upstream.

This leaves you with some quarter of an hour to wait, as it were, for the traffic lights, and it is in that time that each individual Nelson or Hawkins sees his opportunity to outwit the enemy with his brilliant naval tactics.

The object of the exercise is simply for the later-comers to queue-jump for a place in the lock on the earlier arrivals. And when there are more boats waiting around than can possibly get into the lock when it opens – which at weekends is always – there is much to play for in these front-of-lock battles.

Faced with a just-shut lock, the Trog cruiser can do one of several things. The most obvious one is to tie up to the nearest post, switch off the engine, pour out a gin, and wait. This pre-supposes that the Trog cruiser (or T.C.) –

a) knows how to tie up,
b) which end to tie first,
c) expects his engine to restart,
d) can undo whatever hitches or grocer's knots that have been used.

It is a fairly simple and commonsense rule that when going upstream you tie by the bows, or the sharp end, first. The stream is flowing towards you and the tendency of your boat will be to stream with the stream. If you secure by the stern, or blunt end, then the stream will push your bows out and round, first to across-stream and then down-stream, until you end dangling in the rather silly position of facing the wrong way with your back to the lock. Your true Trog will always tie up by the stern, it being so much easier to put a rope round the post from the cockpit. Then, when he swings out, he will try to restore the position by dirty great bursts of engine, plus coarse rudder.

This is fun to watch because one of several things will happen when he is cross-stream. Either the bit of string will break, or the hitch come undone, or the cleat on his boat will give way. He will then shoot, under full power, across the river into the opposite bank, or another boat (whichever comes first). Mum will start to scream, the children to yell, the other Nelsons will curse or shout advice, and the possibilities of the scene become endless. Eventually the dangling bit of string will wrap itself round the prop – the engine will stop dead – and the T.C. will drift off broadside downstream across the bows of an excursion steamer.

There is always just the chance, however, that the mooring rope will hold, and ditto the post and the boat's cleat. In that case the T.C. will make a series of cross-stream bounds, each to the limit of the rope, like a chained dog jumping from its kennel – until it, too, ends facing downstream with the rope so jammed round the post that it will have to be cut loose.

Meanwhile the semi-experienced T.C.s, well knowing what mayhem is likely to be let loose around the mooring posts in the immediate vicinity of the lock-gates, will be engaged in thrilling fleet manoeuvres clear of the danger area. Other knowing ones will be hanging back and watching the lock, because there is no point in showing their hand too soon.

There is another small point worthy of note in the pre-lock ploys. When a lock-full of water starts being dumped into the river below, it rushes out at a fair and turbulent rate through the big gaps in the main gates created by the raising of the panels. This turbulent water has a considerable content

of circular motion, or undertow, so that an unwary boat is not only sucked smartly forward when it expects to be pushed back, but is also turned around. If a rival Trog Captain can be lured to a position adjacent to the lock-gates at a time coincident with this outrush of water, he can dent both his bows and then his stern in the one exciting hydrobatic performance. The same interesting effect is produced inside the lock itself when the upstream water is first allowed to pour in. The initial reaction of the boats is to strain forward, and, if there is no stern line to hold them, they will try to savage the back-end of the boat in front. Furthermore, they will often succeed.

The truly experienced and competent Captain knows all this. He will, therefore, already have quietly tied up to the bank (there is always a tree or a post or a stone or a stick) – bows first – and then by the stern. He will also have sent a reliable scout onto the lock quay-side itself to signal progress. This scout can always be retrieved later as he can merely step back on board at quay level. In the interim he can catch the boat's warps when it enters the lock, and also have time to use the facilities, buy some pop or an ice-cream and enjoy the many Trog happenings inside the lock itself, of which more anon. Fenders can also be put out on both sides of the boat because they are soon going to be very necessary, and long warps of double maximum lock-wall-height checked for free running, placed at both the sharp and blunt ends. The experienced captain can then light his pipe and settle down to watch the main Trog action out in mid-stream.

This will consist of the warring craft turning round each other in ever decreasing circles – the fleet gradually drifting downstream and pausing only to let by the odd T.C. already disabled from the mooring post area. The object of the circling is, of course, like in musical chairs, to be in a position to get into the lock before anyone else – or, alternatively, to make sure that no-one else gets into it at all if you can't.

As in all battles of manoeuvre there will be casualties. Some will be by collision, but most will be by engine failure. Even modern outboards – and most of the T.C. engines will be un-modern outboards – tend to be temperamental and many don't have a gear box or clutch (you go astern by turning the whole contraption round). Throttles can, and do, jam open and jam shut – while many Trogs are not all that clear which way to put the tiller anyway. It is as well to note at this stage that most T.C. Mums never solve this problem. So if you see a T.C. Mum at a tiller make for the shore. Do not argue – do not hang around. Clear the area – downstream if necessary – but go. And if you wonder why so many of the T.Cs. have silly little bulkhead mounted steering wheels and cables rather than a comfortable tiller – you know now.

The battle of manoeuvre will go on for most of the lock cycle. As the disabled boats get carried off downstream reinforcements will arrive, either fresh from triumphs or with bitter revenge from previous lock battles in their hearts. As the boats which worsted them in the last scrap will almost certainly be among those caught out by the shutting of this one, many single ship actions will immediately be renewed. The object of these is to force the other boat into the bank (or if the battle is on the upstream side of the lock – down and across the posts guarding the weir). In the middle of all this excitement the lock gates can often open unnoticed – unnoticed, that is, by all except the non-combatant and experienced captains. These have already received the "readiness" signal from their quay-side scouts and have quietly sidled away from the bank to be in position to slip, at tick-over speed, into the lock as soon as the last "down" boat has left – if not a bit before. They can then ease forward to the departure end of the lock – pick the side on which their scout is already waiting to receive the warps – throw him up the bow warp – throw up the stern warp, and carry on smoking behind a screen of fenders. The ropes are now round a quay bollard and back to the deck, so there is no need even to touch the slimy lock sides or holds – that is if you know how to throw up a long rope.

Back in the battle area there is now real mayhem. All the T.Cs. have noticed that the lock is open and those which happened to be pointing the right way at the time have opened up to full chat and are heading, line abreast, for it. Inevitably this line of boats is going to be at least two boats too wide for the 17 foot bottle-neck ahead, and so the flankers either have to stop, hit the shoulders of the gates, or (more usually) alter course inwards and hope to force all the boats inside them to move over one. As the opposite flanker is doing exactly the same thing, but in the other sense, life becomes critical for the middle boat which is being converged upon from both sides. If he is a big boat and has all his fenders down he will hold straight on and let the others bounce off him. This will throw both sets of boats either side of him out towards the banks, which each flanker will then hit at an angle of attack of about 45 degrees. The centre boat has now only to accelerate to dominate the lock entrance. If the centre boat is a small cruiser, however, he will be well advised, in the squeeze play, to strike his colours and throttle back to drop astern. There will then be – in soccer parlance – a 4:1:1 line-up for the lock, and the rear "1" will always be a river excursion steamer of enormous size and many decks which has already ploughed un-heeded (save by the lock-keeper) through the rearguard of the battle and is quite happy to plough through the van. These river steamers know only one thing about locks – and that is that if the gates are open they go in – and nobody, but nobody, argues with them. One river steamer and you nearly have a fair lockful. The lock-keeper will now re-arrange the Trogs already inside – who, if they have any sense, will hang on like grim death to the steamer sides until the gates are safely shut. But, by this time, some T.Cs. who hadn't got quick warps to the quay top, or to the sideholds before the steamer arrived, are now lying unattached and sideways across the lock and are bleating pitifully. Ropes are being waved and the lock-keeper is telling them what they can do with them. Eventually one of the experienced captains sends his ten year old daughter on board the appropriate T.Cs. to sort things out, and the operation can proceed.

A further word here about engines. If the T.C. outboard has no clutch, then, when the engine is running, the prop is always turning and the T.C. moving remorselessly ahead. As the outboard is also unlikely to have a tick-over much below half throttle, the tendency is for the T.C. to move ahead fairly sharpish. What is needed, however, on coming into and leaving an up-lock, is just enough speed to stem the stream and to make ahead at about a knot or so. Easy to do with a clutch, but there is much incident potential without one.

The clutchless, fast tick-over T.C. has to judge just when to throttle back (in fact to stop the engine) and to glide the rest of the way to the lock walls. This he seldom manages to do – either because he gets it wrong, or because some other T.C. beats him to his chosen space, or gets becalmed across his bows. The T.C. is now adrift and engine-less in the lock and dare not re-start his motor because, as soon as he does, he will shoot ahead at great speed and deal everything else in the lock a severe injury. All he can sensibly do is to hang on to the nearest other boat which is highly likely to be another T.C. in the same pickle. In that case both will drift down out of the lock unless they are thrown a friendly rope by the experienced captain, – or his ten year old daughter.

Now and then the lock-side Trog spotter will be rewarded by the awe-some sight of a T.C. running amok in the lock with a jammed throttle. This situation can only be restored by earthing the plug. But until the T.C. gets around to doing that, the scene can be both gay and animated. On the whole it is best to tow any T.C. prone to such tricks into the lock, horse-drawn – barge fashion, and to tow it out again.

Let us now assume that all is safely gathered into the lock and the gates are shut both ends. Outside those gates the permanent battles of manoeuvre will still be in progress, with mostly a new caste – but our T.C. is, however, and for the moment, insulated and relatively safe inside. He can either be alongside the lock wall, probably holding onto slimy chains as his boat rises to the inrush of water, or be tied alongside another boat which, in turn, is attached in same upward sliding manner to the lock wall. All he now has to do is to sit tight and he will be lifted to the upper level and to freedom.

Unless, that is, he has tied his boat firmly to a wall-side ring, chain or rung halfway up, in which case he is badly placed when the water rises above the points of attachment and he can't free his now submerged pieces of string. You don't believe that can happen, then your first hour or so Trog spotting at a busy lock will correct that view.

Once the lock has waved farewell to its up-river load, it is now open for business in a downstream direction. The same basic situation and war of manoeuvre applies above the lock as the one we have already observed at the lower level. With one important difference. This time the stream is relentlessly carrying the casualties and, indeed, all the T.Cs. down towards the lock and not away from it. Incidentally, it is also carrying them towards the weir for which the lock is a by-pass. The drift, in short, is now towards trouble. This sharpens up the action considerably.

The weirs themselves are sensibly screened by safety posts set close together so that no boat can be swept down between them. That is so (although one or two have contrived to get through somehow), but there is nothing to prevent a T.C. being pinned sideways across the row of weir posts and held firmly there by the dancing waters. Nothing at all. The noise of a Trog Mum on board a boat so pinned is, if anything, louder than that of a dinghy race, and remains so until someone kindly tows them clear.

I will draw a veil over further Trog manoeuvres in water which is carrying them down onto a major fixed obstruction to navigation such as a lock. It is in such conditions that T.C. captains first grasp the fundamental truth that driving a river cruiser isn't just the same as driving a car. In a car, the road stays put. In a boat the road is moving and that, as they discover, is one hell of a difference.

Once inside a "down" lock life is easier because the T.C. comes in at quay level and can readily attach itself prettily and nautically to bollards on the quay side. Since the T.C. is now going downstream it is the stern which must be tied first and the sharp end afterwards. To do it the other way round will be to court the old cross-stream swing again.

There is one snag, however, about being hitched up prettily and nautically to quay-side bollards. That occurs when the water starts to run out of the bath and boat begins to move smartly downwards with the water level. One of two things can then happen. Either the mooring ropes are paid out at either end to allow the boat to descend. Or they aren't. In the latter case the T.C. can be left dangling by its own ropes – a fascinating and rewarding spectacle. The crew is by now on the quayside working like mad trying to lower the boat down by its warps onto full contact with the receding surface of the water. This, to be truthful, they usually achieve before any actual dangling ensues, but this leaves the crew up on the quay and the boat deck six feet or so below them and still going down. Either the warps are now long enough for the crew upstairs to hold onto them from above until the lock is empty, or they aren't. If not, then the T.C. and warps have to be abandoned to the temporary care of a rescue crew, while the real crew walk to the lower bank and ask if they can have their boat back, please. It is a nice point if salvage is claimable. An alternative, of course, is to have ropes long enough to reach from the bottom of the lock up round a quayside bollard and down back to the boat again. Few T.Cs. have such.

Enough then of Trogs in locks. The foregoing is only a sample of what can happen, especially when big hire cruisers are added to the scene. And Hire Cruisers deserve a chapter to themselves.

(P.S. It is Trog Positive to journey an un-necessary yard in any boat . with fenders down. This is one thing which Nelson would never have done – ever.)

2

Hire Cruisers

These come in two main sizes – big and bigger. They are solid lumps of very rugged boat bearing the campaign scars of a lifetime of battle. Usually they have the main cabin at the front and a smaller cabin at the back – the steering being in a sensibly protected position in the middle. Very early on in his Thames experience, the veriest Trog Captain learns to recognise a Hire Cruiser at distant sight and to avoid any provocation which might lead to combat. Next to a Pleasure Steamer or a Thames Tug, the Hire Cruiser is the most daunting adversary on the river. An analogy is a six foot three inch drunken Irish navvy in a Dublin bar where nobody, but nobody argues with Reilly. Unless, of course, it is another six foot three inch drunken Irish navvy.

Hire Cruisers – with their impressive array of big rope fenders (sometimes even motor tyres) are the armoured personnel carriers of the river. They are taken out by a bewildering cross-section of the great British boat-loving public – Trog and non Trog – but mainly very Trog indeed. If one has to generalise, the majority of H.C. crews are either Mum and Dad plus Grandma and up to ten Troglings, or a bevy of assorted and lively young females with two or three very tired looking youths.

The time to be particularly aware of the mayhem potential of H.Cs. is when they are in the lower reaches and on their way upstream. Coming down river and back to their hiring bases (mainly in suburban Surrey/Middlesex) they have inevitably gained some painful knowledge of what a boat can do. But just starting out with a song in their heart and a transistor on the deck for a week's sampling of the brochure joys of exploration into the picturesque by-ways of England's oldest and most historic highway – they are, in a word, a menace.

All hirers, I doubt not, are pre-required to show that they are competent with the engine controls and the wheel, but I have heard doubts very widely expressed about the validity of this test. The fundamental, as I have already said, is for the crews to realise that the river itself is actually in independent motion. Also that the water is deeper in the middle than at the edges – and the bottom of the river can get in the way of the bottom of the boat. I have no religious objections to Hire Cruisers being aground – *au contraire.* But they usually hunt in pairs and one H.C. trying to tow another off the mud is something to give a wide berth to. *En passant,* I would observe that even the simple towing of another boat is far from easy. The towed vehicle tends to swing from side to side and to create an undamped fugoid of wilder and wilder sideways surges. It is not equipped with brakes and will also quickly over-run the tow if the latter slows down too suddenly. So, if ever you see one amateur towing another, take a mental note of the length of the tow-rope and reckon that everything inside its radius measured from the back of the towing vehicle is as potentially lethal as a minefield.

The one thing you can bet that Hire Cruisers have always got is crew. They pour out on deck from the various hatchways and cabin doors on every rumour of an impending crisis – like a lock, of which there are some forty-seven on the Thames.

Now, on any boat, the trouble potential increases directly as the square of the number of inexperienced crew rushing about the deck with ropes and boathooks. This, too, is an axiom which can be written in all notebooks alongside the basic *"Nelson never had an engine".* I am fully aware that in our permissive and liberal society there is no idealogical room for such a reactionary fascist beast as a Captain, but, in any waterborne vehicle capable of independent movement, a Captain there has to be. On an H.C. it can be assumed that the man actually at the wheel imagines he has been so elected by due democratic process. You can also assume he is the only one on board who actually believes that. Practically every H.C., therefore, is a floating republic. The situation in moments of tension, whether caused by or in a lock, or by the approach of a River Steamer, or by the simple desire to pull up alongside the busy landing stage of a pub, is that the Brother at the wheel thinks he is in charge and starts to give orders. It is at this stage that, as we have already noted, he sees himself as a Jack Hawkins figure ("Port Ten – Make Smoke") and wishes to impress with his cool and calm demeanour under pressure and by sure use of terse, appropriate, nautical phrases. Unfortunately, to make himself heard above the transistor pop, he also has to shout – which detracts from the image, and as this invites all the crew to shout back, the wheelman is soon in a minority of one in his belief in the Hawkins syndrome. A parallel with Charlie Drake or Laurel and Hardy comes more readily to mind.

The standard vocal – mostly at "ff" – goes something like this:-

Hawkins:	:	'Make fast forrard. Finished with engines.'

(Together – Crew No1/2/3)

Crew No.1	:	'What?'
Crew No.2	:	'You can't stop here, it says danger.'
Crew No.3 (aft)	:	'I'll tie this rope round that post.'
Crew No.1	:	'Did you say something?'
Hawkins	:	'I said, make fast forrard.'
Crew No.1	:	'What to?'
Hawkins	:	'Tie that bloody rope round that bloody post for God's sake – quick.'
Crew No.2	:	'It says 'Danger'.'
Crew No.3	:	'I've tied my rope already.'
Hawkins	:	'You've what?'
Crew No.3	:	'Like I said, I've tied the back rope.'
Hawkins	:	'Then untie it sharpish.'
Crew No.4	:	'Here's the boathook.'
Hawkins	:	'Give it to Jill up front and let her grab that ring. Jill, grab the ring with the boat-book.'
Crew No.5	:	'What ring?'
Hawkins	:	'Have you untied that rope at the back yet?'
Crew No.3	:	The rope's in a robble.
Hawkins	:	'I can't make the engine start again – someone come and start the engine.'
Crew No.1	:	'Have you turned on the petrol?'
Crew No.5	:	'I can see the ring, but I can't reach it. Why don't you keep the boat still?'
Hawkins	:	'Can someone lasso the post up front with the rope while we start the engine? And turn off that stinking radio.'
Crew No.5	:	'I've got the ring on the boathook.'
Hawkins	:	'Then pull the front in to the post.'
Crew No.5	:	'I can't. The boat's trying to swing the other way.'
Hawkins	:	'Then hang on. Fred give Jill a hand with the boathook.'
Crew No.4	:	'For gawd's sake..... Oh blimy!'
Hawkins	:	'What the hell's happened now?'

Crew No.4 : 'The boathook's gone – it's hanging from that bloody stupid ring of yours.'

Crew No.1 : 'I reckon we should start the engine – untie the back and shove off.'

Crew No.4 : 'Then what about the boathook?'

Crew No.3 : 'I can't undo my rope from the post, but I can undo it from the boat.'

Hawkins : 'We've got the engine going. Cast off aft.'

Crew No.3 : 'Is that me?'

Hawkins : 'Yes – at the back. Let go.'

Crew No.3 : 'But we'll leave the rope behind.'

Crew No.4 : 'And the boathook.'

Hawkins : 'Cast off, you stupid b..... – full ahead – Oh mi gawd!'

Crew No.2 : 'I told you it said danger.'

When the H.C. crew is Dad and Mum and Grandma plus Troglings, the actual dialogue is somewhat different, but the net result is about the same – with hysterics, tears and a large splash ("Emma's fallen off") added – which brings me nicely to the subject of boathooks.

In the right hands and at the right time the boathook can be a useful tool, For picking up a mooring, or for holding on close alongside something for a moment while a warp is secured – it can't be beaten. It also comes in handy for fishing a trailing rope out of the water, or for re-capturing a halliard flying in the wind. Now and then it represents the initial hope of raking in a bucket or a small crew member kicked off the foredeck. But as a substitute for basic motive power or an additional control surface it is a non-starter. Most Trog Captains try to use it in the latter role. This leads them to the situation we have already seen in the Hire Cruiser, when the simple choice facing the wielder is whether to stay with the boathook or with the boat.

The power exerted by moving water – be it tide or river current – on a heavy boat, once the pressure gets a grip on the hull, is beyond that of a boathook and a pair of arms. The boat will still go on swinging cross-tide to down-tide, and as the force on the hook is then considerable, there is little hope of disentangling it from whatever it has been inserted into. That is why, at so many river locks and tidal moorings, you can see abandoned boathooks dangling from posts or floating away down-tide, while frantic attempts are made to launch a rescue dinghy.

I recall, many years ago now, being on a rich friend's 100 foot twin diesel motor cruiser which we were taking up the Seine. It was decided to spend. the fast-falling night lying between two tall mid-stream pylons – some 200 ft apart. The simple plan of action was to motor gently up into the current until the sharp end was nudging the up-stream pylon and secure a long 150 ft warp to it. We would then lay back on the stream to the second pylon, make the blunt end fast to it, and finally adjust the warps until we were moored fore and aft snug between the two posts. The first part worked fine. The front warp was hitched to the post (we hadn't a rope long enough to run it through the rung and lead it back on itself) and, with a touch of engines astern, we started to drift back, paying out rope over the bows as we went. Unhappily the current didn't actually carry us straight back to the second pylon – it took a big curve towards the bank instead. As a result, laying back on the warp failed to take us to the post, but to a spot some ten or fifteen yards to one side. There then followed the most un-Hawkins-like playing of tunes on the two engines – ahead on one – astern on the other – aimed at coaxing us by sideways jerks over that ten yards or so to the post. At this stage much free advice was being tendered to our Captain – mine being limited to the thought that it might be easier to launch the dinghy from the davits and row the rope across. But he was now in full Hawkins, and was reinforced in this by a lucky surge that took us for a moment within a few feet of the pylon. It was already nearly dark and word had spread through the little French village on the bank that there was a 'happening' out on the river. An admiring crowd began to gather on the landing stage and, I was later told, they even rang the church bell so that no-one would miss the show. Shouts in fluent French were drifting on the twilight air as we came near enough to the pylon for the boat's crewman to grab a mooring ring with the boathook. The boat then began to drift away again – aided by a splendid burst of engine which our Captain later proved mathematically to me on a bit of paper, was bound to check the swing and bring the stern back close to the post. The theory, I doubt not, was faultless. The fact was that the boat shied away even faster, and the crewman now had to face the classic boathook situation. He chose to remain with the boathook. By the time the boat was back on station, ten yards from the pylon, he was hanging onto the boathook with his legs wrapped round the pylon. A cheer broke out from the bank as someone brought up a car and illuminated the scene with a spotlamp. Other cars arrived and soon there were headlights all round while the French became more fluent as the inn-keeper set up a waiter-service to the crown on the stage. There were more cheers as the crewman achieved the top of the post and sat on it. It was just about now that the rope tying us to the forward pylon dipped under the water and snagged on something on the river bed. Activity was transferred to the sharp end and to wild swingings to free the warp – which only snagged it worse. The crewman was now getting vocal in Polish – because he happened to be a Pole.

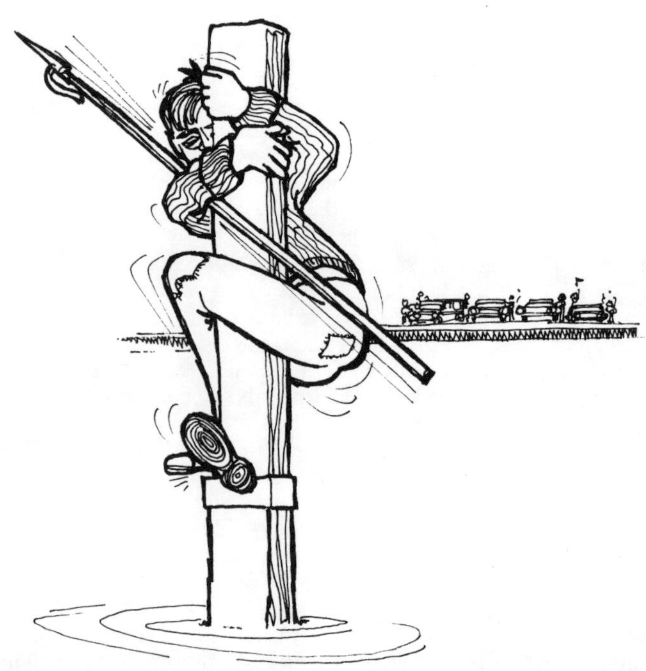

Something clearly had to be done – and the something was to cut the forward warp as close to the underwater snags as possible and motor back to the crewman's pylon – where he was persuaded to clamber down from his perch and to jump onto the deck. He misssd, but grabbed a rail and was, to the loudest cheer of the night, hauled back on board and given a hot rum.

We then slunk away upstream and round the next bend. The quay-side cars accompanied us like vultures on the riverside road. Then they all stopped and turned their lights onto a trot of normal and empty mooring buoys – which is what they'd been trying to tell us about all along. We picked one up and saw off the rest of the rum. Next day – and – for the first and last time that trip – we were astir at dawn. We slunk back to the pylons – retrieved the ignominious dangling boathook – unsnagged the remainder of the warp – and were away into the pearly mist.

I will resist the temptation to follow this epic journey further and to describe what can happen in a French lock to a British pleasure boat surrounded by Seine barges. But if any reader likes to find out at first hand I would give only one tip – stack a liberal supply of bottles of wine on deck and hand them round to everyone in sight. You may then survive.

There is one final but important aspect of river life – we are now back on the Thames – which I would like to touch on, and that is coming alongside the landing stage of a pub.

The usual drinking hours situation facing a Trog Captain who only wants to be there for the beer, is that every inch of the landing stage is already covered by boats whose crews are already visible sitting in the pub's olde worlde riverside garden – foaming tankards in hand. They are very very smug indeed because they know that you are now likely to provide them with the splendid diversion which was all they needed to be truly content. I doubt if there is any more potential situation from Lechlade to Teddington.

The beer-less T.C. will, if he is sensible, take his boat round in a gentle orbit while he weighs up the position. What, he wonders, would Hawkins do? Undoubtedly Hawkins would go downstream of the stage, turn into the current, and come up gently alongside the most convenient of the tied-up boats – all fenders down on the appropriate side. He and his crew would then hold on fore and aft, while hitching up the sharp end and then the blunt end to convenient and reliable projections on the other boat's deck – like cleats. He would then go nonchalantly ashore by clambering over the foredeck of the inner boat and make the appropriate gesture to the assembled tankard holders whose rage at being robbed of their sport would be ill concealed.

That is the Hawkins' solution. What your actual T.C. will almost certainly do is to select a bit of unoccupied bank adjacent to the beer garden clear of the crowded landing stage and ram it with his bows. He will then jump ashore over said bows and yell for warps to be passed to him both from the front of his boat and from the back. There will be no warps. He will then demand the boathook and go through the boathook ploy – choosing, in final confrontation, to stay on the bank while boat and crew go adrift. I will spare you the rest, but, in the end – amid the tapping of appreciative beer-mugs – he will still finish up tied outside another boat.

T.C. and crew will just be getting their blushing faces into their first pint when the Trog Captain belonging to the boat our T.C. is tied up to, will ostentatiously stand up and announce that he has to be on his way and will the owner of the *Chertsey Queen* please now prepare to detach himself from the *Pride of Pentonhook,* which is otherwise and in all respects, ready for sea. The *Chertsey Queen* can now do one of three things:-

a) Take no notice (unrewarding – everyone in the beer garden knows who brought *Chertsey Queen* and are looking forward very much to episode two).

b) Leave the beer – go back on board – cast off – do another circuit and then try to re-park very publicly in the tight vacant space left by the *Pride of Pentonhook.*

c) Say "All right – I'll let you out ahead and pass my forward warp round your stern as you go and then pull my boat in to the stage when you've gone".

Alternative (b) is clearly a potential – nay certain – repeat disaster, so alternative (c) is quickly selected to the lip-licking satisfaction of all present.

The audience can now settle down in anticipatory glee for a completely new version of the Riverside Follies. As a curtain raiser a *Chertsey Queen* crew member goes back on board to undo his stern line and throw it to his Captain on shore. It falls in the river. This is partly because it is thrown badly and mainly because it isn't long enough. To throw a rope it must be loosely coiled in generous loops – and then the coil split into two halves – one set held in the right hand the remainder in the left. The right hand coils are then thrown – and a split second later the left hand coils are released and will pay out nicely and impressively. Throw the whole rope and the betting is it won't go two yards. It doesn't – and the *Queen's* crewman has to drag its sopping length back while his unattached stern is drifted slowly out on a back-eddy. The *Queen's* boat-to-shore distance is now beyond the scope of the after warp, and another bit of rope has to be found and tied on. There is discussion as to what is the proper bend to join two unequal diameter ropes together – but this is a waste of time because it will end as a granny knot – which it does.

By this time the *P. of P.'s* Captain is, with exaggerated patience and bogus cameraderie, himself holding the *Queen's* stern by boathook and is visibly dallying with the idea of casting off and leaving the *Queen* and its crew of one adrift in midstream. The audience holds its breath – will he – won't he? He has game, set and match in his grasp. With a patient and self-sacrificing smile, he passes up the chance.

So eventually *Chertsey Queen* has a line of sorts to her Captain who is standing on the landing stage holding both bits of string. He hitches the stern one round a bollard – which is fair enough – and with the help of the *Pride's* Captain they pass the forward line right round the *Pride* and behind her and back to the stage. All obstructions removed, the *Pride* is now clear to go ahead and out. The *Queen's* Captain then only has to pull in both his warps to have his boat alongside. The audience sighs its disappointment, the fun is now over and back to the beer.

It is at this juncture that the *Queen* plays her trump card. The *P. of P.*, with full roar of engine ahead, is shooting away from the quay. The startled Captain of the *Chertsey Queen* drops his long forward warp which snags round the *P. of P.'s* retreating stern rail – tugging the *Queen* after it. The *Queen's* stern line granny-knot parts under the jerk – and the *Pride of Pentonhook* with the *Chertsey Queen* in tow, heads out to mid-river. The *Pride's* Captain in panic clears the tow line from his stern rail and drops it overboard straight into his own prop. A quick underwater flurry of ten turns of rope round the prop-shaft – the *Pride's* engine stops dead – and the two drifting boats dwindle slowly downstream as the audience rises in grateful tribute.

3

The Broads

However strongly one advances the case for the Thames Hire Cruiser as reaching, from time to time, the heights of inland waterway Troggery – one is very conscious that, in a head-to-head encounter, the patrons of the Norfolk Broads would probably win any three of a five test series by an innings – or, alternatively, by 6:1, 6:1, 6:0, or by 9 up and 8 to play.

In truth, The Broads produces a different class of game. Individual ploys at Thames locks can be breathtaking in their genius, but for solid drilled reliable steam-roller performance which never falls below par, never misses a half volley outside the off-stump or a 12 inch putt, and never serves a double fault – the Broads are out on their own.

On the Thames the Hire Cruiser is in the minority and its level of performance is watered down by many untalented amateurs. On the Broads practically every floating device is on hire, and, furthermore, a very high percentage of them is equipped with sails – with which whole new horizons of inspiration and achievement are within the reach of all. Also, the density of population per boat is uniformly high, and you will recall that a ship's confusion factor varies as the square of the number of its crew.

There are three kinds of Hire Cruiser on the Broads – those with only sails, those with sails plus an auxilliary engine, and motor boats. On the Thames, the only sails you see belong to dinghies which are nearly always competently conducted. On the Broads you get socking great shallow-draft sailing yachts of which, perhaps, one in four is under control.

The Broads themselves are, in effect, a collection of lakes linked by a maze of quite narrow and shallow rivers. The rivers are spanned at frequent intervals by bridges low enough to take off masts – nay low enough to take off foredeck crew, and do so year after year, after year. The flow of the rivers is partially tidal – the tide rise increasing with nearness to the sea. If you particularly want to make a name for yourself you can go through the approaches that liberate you into the harbours of Yarmouth and Lowestoft. There you will encounter real water that moves about in a very determined way, and also real iron-type ships that don't mind much if you hit them or not. I recall once standing in Yarmouth on the deck of a little motor cabin cruiser I then owned, and which – after some minor excitements – I had safely tied up. Then, suddenly, there was this Broad's Sailer – main sheet tight in, and mainsail taut – dead across a force 4 wind and the whole boat dead across the ebb tide. It was heeling down-wind and down-tide and making an impressive speed broadside on across the harbour, while several of the crew alternatively tried to grab a mooring and to drop an anchor, with several more crew pushing and pulling the tiller – all, as far as I could see, with nil effect all round. It was a fascinating sight because they were being carried right onto the fat stern of a large moored fishing vessel and no-one was wearing life-jackets. Eventually they hit the fishing vessel with a lovely crunch – ropes were thrown by a bored fisherman who leaned over and freed the mainsheet and let them tie up alongside for a breather.

The moral of this is that if you are not used to the sea – then for Gawd's sake stay on the Broads side of the bridge or lock, like the guide books say. It is not as if there is any lack of incident potential on the Broads side of the out-of-bounds. There is all that the Thames offers with the infinite possibilities inherent in your actual sails as an added extra.

Consider what the average Broads sailor has available to perpetrate mayhem with. He has a mainsail (which is pulled up the mast by a rope called a halliard) and across whose foot is a substantial plank of wood or metal called a boom. From the rear or aft end of the boom he has some complicated bits of string (the mainsheet) which can either pay the boom out until it is nearly at right angles to the fore and aft line of the boat – or can pull it in until the boom (and sail) are, themselves, lying in a fore and aft line. Roughly speaking, the closer into the wind he is trying to sail, the more he wants the boom fore and aft – and the broader the wind gets to the side – the more he wants to let the sail out. Eventually – in theory – when the wind is blowing from behind, the sail can go out to 60 degrees or so, but this only works comfortably if the wind stays exactly put and so does the ship's direction. As this never happens, what is now going to occur to our friend is called a "gybe", which can be fun. There he is, standing proud and erect in the cockpit, running before a nice wind – mainsail right out on the starboard side – water creaming under his bows, the song of the birds in his ears and everyone ahead of him is already beginning to take shelter or jumping onto the bank.

Any moment now the wind relative to his boat is going to shift, because he is coming towards a gentle right hand curve in the river and he is going to have to alter course to follow it. And when he does, the wind is going to stop filling his sail from behind and begin to hit it a little from the front. The whole contraption will then whip over, like the kick of a mule, from full out to starboard to full out to port and this whole contraption will include the so-solid boom, which will, en passant, knock him out cold – or overboard – or both. By the time help has arrived from the cabin and he has either drowned or struggled ashore – the boat will have charged on with a free tiller and gybing merrily (if the mast and rigging stand up) until it hits something like the bank or another boat, which is why everyone for a quarter of a mile down-wind of him has scrambled clear a long time since.

So – let no-one rejoice when they have a good following wind – but, instead, grow pale and consider whether the mainsail should not be let

MASTER MARINER

down altogether in favour of proceeding on just the front sail which is called a fore-sail – or, by most people, a jib – of which more will follow.

Which brings me on to the fact that most sailing yachts have two sails – and these have to be hauled up and down on halliards, and are controlled by these bits of string called sheets. This nomenclature is perplexing to many people who think "sheets" are sails – whereas they are ropes controlling sails.

The pulling up and pulling down of the sails on the Broads can give endless joy to the onlooker. Many Broads boats are what are called gaff rigged and this gives the would-be Hornblower yet another bit of string to play with. In a gaff rig, the mainsail does not come to a point at the top of mast (as with a Bermuda sail), but is more square in shape and has a spar running along the top, which spar (or gaff) cocks up at an angle and is controlled by a peak halliard running from the end of the gaff to the mast and then down. By pulling in the peak halliard you can jerk the gaff higher and tauter and so tighten the sail and take its weight as it lies all crinkled between the gaff at the top and the boom at the foot, or bottom. This stops the sail sagging away sloppily to leeward from about halfway up – or such is the theory. But whether you have a gaff or a Bermuda (non-gaff) rig, you have the same initial problem – getting the thing up. Sails have a life and a will of their own, and most of the bits of rope which attach to them are so evil that some Broads Trogs try to exorcise them by burning candles and dancing widdershins on Midsummer nights.

So there you are – in the *"Beauty of Wroxham"* – tied to spikes in the bank off a Broad by bits of rope at each end as per the Thames – or even lying to a mud weight, which is the Broads version of an anchor. This is a lump of something heavy attached to a rope or chain and which you heave over the front end to make you stay put. It will do this in a Broad and will actually slow your downstream drift in a river. Anyway, it is a splendid day, and now is the time to hoist sail and be off to the many adventures which some sixth sense tells you are soon to be yours. In fact, very soon. The wind is quite light off-shore (or off-bank) – and you propose to glide away under its power to knowing nods of approval from the two small boys and four cows who are your only audience – for the time being. Right away you have a decision to make. You have two sails – the little one at the front and the big one. Which to put up first? The little one, you reckon, is the lesser problem and had better wait till the boat is moving and the main crisis past. So – "up with the main", you say to yourself as you undo the bits of string tying the sail in its neat parcel along the boom. A quick down haul on the main halliard and up she goes. Well – up she goes for the first yard or so – when the sail bellies out in the wind and the pressure causes the slides to jam in the mast groove – or the rings to jam against the mast – whichever way your sail happens to be attached. Anyway, it sticks quarter way up and you can't shift it. So – tie it off and get to the cockpit to unfasten the main sheet, which you should have done as item number one, and this allows the sail and boom to swing free with the wind and take the pressure off the slides. By this time – if you were tied to the bank you no longer are, because even a quarter sail full of broadside wind is a pretty powerful motive force. Or, if you were on a mud weight, you have swung round and are now lying to wind with the sail flapping and cracking, but actually doing no harm at all. The audience is now four small boys and others are hurrying up with that instinct which all the locals have for a happening about to happen. They usually, on any Broad, have a choice of several at any one time, but are very clever at picking the most spectacular one for their patronage. It is a kind of Norfolk ESP. So, whenever you see your bankside audience growing, stop whatever it is you are doing, revert to a state of rest if you can, furl the sails and start the motor. If you haven't a motor then get out the quant – which is a sort of punt pole and is the traditional auxilliary power of the Broads – and quant yourself away with dignity.

In passing I may mention that quanting – like punting – frequently propounds the old boathook problem of whether to stay with the pole or with the boat. It is often a nice decision, but since the Broads are mostly shallow and quants are precious, the bias is towards staying with the pole.

However, back on the *Beauty of Wroxham,* if you were on a mud weight, all will now be well because your partly filled sail put you into wind before it started to flap – which is where you should have been in the first place before you touched the main halliard. You could have achieved this state of grace by hauling up the foresail first with the sheets free, and then tightening up. This would have kept you riding into wind, or near enough. The main could then have been hoisted at leisure (with mainsheet free) – the mud weight pulled up – and by playing the sheets a bit and with help from the tiller, you could have turned and sailed into the dawn. The audience would have been furious, but generous in its appreciation, as it left on the double to visit the motor cruiser with its stub mast stuck under the bridge just along the nearby river.

If, however, you had started your day tied to the bank and no longer are, you will by now be hard aground amid the reeds on the opposite, or lee bank of the Broad and it is going to take an awful lot of quanting to get you off again.

By this time the perceptive reader will be alive to the happening possibilities of the contiguity of a Trog-crew and sails – whether gaff or other – and will have realised that the stronger the wind the more awesome and audience-worthy will be the happening.

For a week of splendid relaxation on the Broads I suggest you collect your hire boat from whichever yard – check your food stores – and then carefully, and slowly motor to the nearest popular Broad, and to the jetty of an abutting pub and STAY THERE. Do not touch the sails – do not go under any bridges – do not pass go – do not collect £200 – but just stop. You can then put out every fender you've got and lounge about the deck, or in the pub garden, or on the jetty, with an air of great authority and competence and enjoy, with a superior smile, the entertainment which will be freely provided non-stop throughout the hours of daylight. Do not (R) not attempt to provide any entertainment of your own. If your ringside seat is near the entrance to the Broad, so much the better. You will be able to watch each Trog boat motor or quant in and visibly respond to the challenge of the sight of the expanse of water. The crew will start pulling on halliards and untying their sails and saying happily, "just the place for a go". At this stage, muster all hands on deck and assume nonchalant attitudes, and wait for it. If the new arrival is gently held on motor, or by jib, into the wind and the main sail is smoothly hoisted with free sheets, and the boat then turned onto a reach (wind from the side), you are in the presence of non-Trogs and can go back to your drinking. This will be rare. But, when you see (and hear) four people on the main halliard, and the mainsail stick halfway up, and the boat then plunge about with the gaff drooping, and the sail twisted away to leeward, you will know that the curtain is about to go up.

It is a fact of life that a gaff-rigged boat, with the peak halliard not properly adjusted and the top of the sail leaning well away from the mast, is a real brute to steer. In fact, it won't. And if there is no foresail up – which there probably won't be – it is going to be pretty nigh impossible to put the boat about, ie to turn it round and go the other way.

What will happen is that the boat will – and you can rely on this – sail at reasonable speed on a reach and will continue to do this on its own chosen course no matter what antics are performed on the tiller. As the Broad, however spacious, is finite in size, there will be a moment when it runs out of water and tries to climb onto the shore. It is this moment you must not miss. With practice you can estimate to a yard where it will strike and can have your glasses or telescope ready trained on the spot. You can bet on it having a clear run across the Broad. All the other Trog boats will be well aware – mostly from experience – just what is happening, and will have cleared the track. They, too, will have sent below for their spy-glasses. The last to appreciate the true position will be the Trog crew. It will take several hundred yards of lively sailing before it dawns on them that they are going to maintain course and speed until the bitter and predictable end. It is instructive to watch this dawning intelligence. The first person to get a clue is the helmsman who decides to make a small manoeuvre and finds he can't. You can see bigger and bigger swings of the tiller, followed by his shout of "I can't steer her" or "the rudder's jammed" or other similar noises. This alarm causes a committee meeting in the cockpit and everyone then has to have a go to show the helmsman how simple it all is really. Afterwards there is another and clearly more lively committee meeting as the shore becomes more distinctly visible. At this stage someone will say, "let's get that bloody sail down again", and, to be honestly factual, this they might just manage to do – in light airs. If the wind is of reasonable strength, however, and remembering that the boat is more or less side on to it – and so is the well-filled sail – and that the boat cannot be brought up into the wind on account of it is happy and set where it is – the betting is they can't do it. With about twenty yards to go, someone might get as far as disconnecting the sail by freeing the main-sheet completely and letting the sail and boom go right out – which takes the boat "out of gear" as it were – but don't worry, they have left this far too late.

Just before the boat hits the shore, you may well be rewarded by the sight of one of the crew running up the deck holding a tiny fender on a long piece of string and trying to dangle it protectively over the bows. This will make no odds whatever because the bows will rise up on the shallowing mud and the keel will cut a nice channel as it shoots up through the reeds and reaches out over the pastureland beyond. He of the fender will also now be in the pasture – having been deposited there by the inertia attendent upon the boat's abrupt halt. The chances are he will never get back on board because the boat is several feet above him with no hand-holds. The chances also are that the boat will remain where it is for a long time to come because it will be very firmly in some very sticky and adhesive mud, and this for much of its length.

The word will spread that tugs are being sent for – and tugs are what are going to be needed. Later – after opening time, and if you have a dinghy – you might care to row some supplies across – or even sell them at a small profit. By then – with luck – they may actually have got the sail down.

4

The Broads *(continued)*

The Trog potential on the Broads merits – demands – a second chapter – and this is it.

For maximum enjoyment of the plight of others, which is roughly what this book, and a large lump of all life, is all about, there are places on the Broads in which it is very bliss to be alive. The junction of the rivers Bure and Yare at Breydon Water, on the north west border of Yarmouth, is such a place.

It is here that Broad's yachts and cruisers transfer from the Northern Broads to the Southern by coming down the Bure to Yarmouth Yacht Station and then turning right, via a bottleneck, into Breydon Water, which is a large expanse of lightly covered mud through the middle of which flows the Yare from the general direction of Norwich.

There are a number of factors which contribute to spectator interest in the area of the Yarmouth Yacht Station, which is the focus of Bure-Yare junction happenings. The first is that the rivers are quite heavily tidal; the second is that there are mud-banks and shoals everywhere, and especially near the Yacht Station; the third is that the Yare is used by commercial sea-going ships which go up to Norwich; the fourth is that there are low bridges; the fifth is that the transition from Bure to Yare – either way – should only be done at low tide slack water; the sixth is that the river channels are very narrow, and the seventh is that, for the last five miles or more of the Bure, there isn't anywhere else to moor until you reach the Yarmouth Yacht Station. The point of no return slips by without any immediate warning of the fact that "no-return" can mean just what it says.

So – taken all in all – it can be argued that the banks near the Bure-Yare junction should be subject to entertainment tax, or to special VAT, which move would be unpopular with the citizens of Yarmouth who, for lo these many years, have regarded this spot as providing a free open-air theatre comparable only to the Palladium.

Experienced Trog-Spotters will have already realised – along with the citizens of Yarmouth – that the Trog boats, in order to reach the famous junction at slack water (low), will have to come down the Bure on the ebb; that there are several bridges at the end of that heady run, and that it is advisable to stop before reaching the first of those bridges on account of the mast hitting it.

One set of pilot's notes which I have read says, "navigation through Yarmouth needs care, but is not difficult or dangerous if simple rules are observed". It then goes on for a luscious page and a half emphasising how simple those rules are and with potential disaster lightly touched on in every paragraph. There is one which tells how to use a mud-bank to help swing a boat's bows into the tide. Another admits there is some disadvantage when the yacht lowers its mast because it might then find it "difficult to sail".

As far as the eager spectator is concerned, what he can expect to see most often is a yacht coming down the Bure on the ebb and with a waterborne speed over the central mud channel of some three or four knots, plus whatever additional urge it is getting from its sails. In the cockpit will be a man who will, by this time, be actually jumping up and down at the exciting thought of the bridges and the realisation that before he gets to them he must have contrived to turn the boat round in a narrow mud-bank ridden channel, or have got the sails off and the mast (and the speed) down, or have otherwise stopped a device which has no actual pedal marked "brake". His excitement will be shared by his crew, each of whom will have worked out a different and mutually exclusive solution to the problem and be independently administering it. At some stage you can rely that someone will throw over the mud weight, whose continued attachment to the boat will then depend on a number of variables like the boat's speed, what the weight snags against in the mud, and the breaking strain of its rope or chain, and/or the mooring cleat.

The factor, however, which will most interest the absorbed Trog Spotter, is the actual speed at which the boat will finally hit the mud, or bridge – and, if the mud, whether it will be a channel shoal or a deliberately contrived collision with the bank. This speed of impact is important because it alone will decide how many of the crew will actually go overboard. It will also decide how far whoever is on the foredeck at the time will carry in free flight before he hits the water or mud. The Guinness Book does not list the actual record, but aged locals only bother to applaud for a "throw" in excess of ten yards.

Now and then the Trog Spotter will be rewarded by the arrival, at smartish lick down-tide, of a Captain who has already frozen onto the controls and will clearly stay frozen until the first bridge. One supposes that he hopes that it will go away, or that the mast will, in the pinch, go under it, or that, in any event, it won't break, or that someone will fend off with the quant. He will be wrong on all counts.

Now, Broad's yachts have a mast which swings on a pivot. The swinging is helped by a counterweight at the foot, and the whole is kept in place, when upright, by a locking pin or cotter or similar device. This means that the mast can be started on its way down by a push back from ahead, and the rate of descent controlled from in front via the (detached) forestay, and from aft by someone taking the weight on upraised palms when the mast gets near the horizontal. The assumption is that the mainsail has already been lowered.

I tell you all this just to make the point that lowering the mast takes time, and that the onlooker can soon – from the much practice offered – form an excellent judgement as to whether the operation has been started in good time in relation to the speed of the ebb and the proximity of the bridge, or not. Usually not. There then follows a cliff-hanger sequence – with the helmsman dancing up and down and various crew calling out to "slow her down" – especially those actually working on the mast who will be casting calculating glances at the rapidly narrowing gap between them and the bridge. They know that, on the foredeck, they are the exposed and expendable troops.

About now betting can break out among Yarmouth locals which will give you a good guide as to eventual outcome. The usual "favourite" is that the skipper will, at the last moment, opt for the bank, with the results already mentioned. Such a decision wins for him the whistles of derision one hears at football matches when there is a long safety pass back to the goalkeeper. Now and then – as in the "frozen on the controls" case – the incident comes to its natural thrilling climax and this can be of wide general interest if, at the moment of mast/bridge impact, the mast was already unpinned ready for lowering. The betting then concentrates on the stage at which all hands will abandon ship – voluntarily or involuntarily.

In the waterfront pubs of Yarmouth, splendid stories are told of past glories at the first bridge. These get more exciting as the night wears on, and one of the best concerns the chap who was in a losing battle to get the mast down before the final crunch. He had, the story goes, unfastened the fore-stay and was about to push the mast backwards while controlling its descent rate by bracing his feet against the counter-weight. He had, thus, achieved what, in golf terms, would be called Position A, and had done so at the moment when the mast struck the bridge with the full impact force of a spring ebb and a 30 foot boat behind it. The mast and counterweight were now converted into a vertical version of that ancient engine of war which used to hurl stones at beleaguered castles. The initial rate of foredeck crew velocity was controlled partly by the laws of the lever ("give me a fulcrum...") and partly by the statement $E=MV^2$ when M = the mass of the counterweight and V = the impact velocity of the mast on the bridge as finally transmitted via the man's feet. The resultant, I am told, was a flat trajectory – more that of No.1 iron than a 3 wood, which took the foredeck hand under the bridge and on to a landing place which varies, with the lateness of the evening, from a low of Vauxhall Station to a high of North Quay.

I can hold out few hopes to Trog Spotters at the Junction that they will ever personally see such a memorable sight, but they will surely see enough to realise that such a thing is theoretically on – and, of course, under Murphy's Law, if a thing is possible, then sooner or later, it is certain to happen.

The nearest approach to such a catapult-effect, which the onlooker is actually likely to see, will come, however, from well judged use of the mud weight. If this is thrown out forward when the boat is moving briskly on the ebb, and if the weight holds firm in any of the wreckage with which the Bure bottom is bestrewn, and if the attachment from weight to boat holds out, then the result can be quite picturesque.

The boat will decellerate from some 4 knots to nil over a period of milliseconds, the bows will be turned through an initial 90 degrees, and the blunt end will whip round after it – probably striking mud at the moment of peak "g". At this point anything in or on the boat which is not lashed down – including and especially the crew – will leave the place where they were and journey to some other place, clocking a very creditable time for the journey.

All this splendour is on offer in addition to the mundane norm of mooring incident ("I told you the rope wasn't tied to anything") and routine groundings on the shoals. In a quiet way, few things are more satisfying than watching attempts to quant a boat off the mud when all the quant pole does is, itself, to go deeper and deeper into mud, thus providing no equal and opposite reaction with which to propel the boat. There is, in fact, little option but for someone to go over the side and try to wade through the nice warm goo – dragging the yacht behind them.

So, as you will now realise, a splendid holiday can be enjoyed merely by taking rooms in Yarmouth and going out daily to the Bure/Yare junction an hour before low tide. Or, for a change, you can take station the other side of the bridges from the Yacht Station and observe the boats coming from Norwich across Breydon Water and intending to go up the Bure towards Acle and the North Broads. Here the problem has commercial sea-going ships added – like the blue whitener. It is also the patrol area for the "rescue" launch which picks people out of the drink, plucks stranded yachts off the mud, and at a pinch, and a passing of currency, will tow the faint-hearted from the Yacht Station round to Breydon Water.

Breydon Water is a spectator-sport joy in its own right. The brochure pictures show it as a placid lake on which boats do gently sail into the softly setting sun. And, when the tide is in, it can sometimes even look like that. There are also pretty posts sticking out across the middle which are useful in that they tell you exactly how far you have still got to go, from where you are currently stuck, to water deep enough to float in again.

It should be revealed at this stage that, when they settle on the mud, Broad's yachts will lean over further and further to one side or the other, because they have a single fin keel sticking out of their bottom and, not surprisingly, cannot balance on it when aground. Unless a prop or support is arranged for the side towards which the boat is tilting – then it will tilt one hell of a lot. Many Troggers never latch onto the fact that the tide really does go up and down, and that all is not deep water that glistens. It is on Breydon Water that many of them discover such facts of life for the first time, and their reactions vary as the distance they are from the channel markers when the discovery is made.

Picture the happy Trog crew sailing across Breydon from Norwich way, and making for the Bure. They have worked out the time of low water at the Yacht Station and are being very nautical about it indeed. "We'll take the last of the ebb down the Yare – tie up, and then round the junction at low to catch the first of the flood up the Bure" they chant to each other. They like the sound of it, and so they chant it again. Hawkins and Hornblower would, they feel, have approved the ring of such seamanlike planning. "We'll be at the Stracey Arms by opening time," adds the skipper, looking at the chart on which vital navigational information, such as where the pubs are, is all marked and annotated. This announcement is greeted with cheers and cries of "splice the mainbrace". In fact they are not going to splice any mainbrace that day at all, because of two things:- they have already drunk all the ship's beer and the last of the ebb on the Yare is not the same thing as the first of the flood up the Bure. It ought to be – but it isn't. The Yare starts to flood first by a variable, but real margin.

They have – and who can blame them – arrived at Breydon in bags of time to have a nice morale-building sail before facing the rigours of the junction. And so they do – for all of 100 yards outside those pretty posts. They cut through the placid, inviting, deceitful waters with a song in their hearts, until someone says, "I think we've stopped moving" – which they have. So, out with the quant – which finds no bottom in the goo and it takes three people to pluck it out again. By this time, land – or rather mud –

is springing up all around and, almost in a flash, mud *is* actually all around and the boat is heeled over on it so that the deck is steep like the side of a house and the cabin uninhabitable. There is no more depressing sight than a boat lying heeled in acres of mud, far removed from the narrow central channel of black water which oozes drearily across the flats. Other boats go up and down that channel – and, in passing, gesticulate – wave and fetch other people up on deck to look at that boat over there that ran out of water. But, with any luck they'll be out of their public humiliation in seven hours – three to reach dead low and four for enough water to come back to float in. Then, if they have an engine, they could still hope to make against the Yare flood tide, but this would put them at the junction with the Bure flood swirling under the bridges, which is not recommended – ah well – back into the Yare proper and tomorrow is another day.

So – for the notebook – never take a short cut or go for a happy sail outside a marked channel on a falling tide – not even when you think you know the area. I reckon, for example, that I know Chichester harbour pretty well and I was happily tacking back and forth across a channel with the ebb and lengthening my tacks by going outside it on the echo-sounder until it read 5 ft (I drew 3 ft) before going about. But there was this three foot rising bank across me on the next tack – and there I was for eight hours. Prompt drill, however, saved the crew. We were in the dinghy like a flash and pulling away for the shore and a pub while there was still enough water to row in. We slunk in and around that pub all the remaining hours of that daylight while friends of ours sailed past hither and yon in the channel and rehearsed throw-away sentences for our next meeting – like "What odd places you pick to dry out". There is always this heavy pretence on both sides that of course you went aground deliberately for some good housekeeping reason – like scraping the bottom. So the required reply is, "Yes – we thought we'd hit the prop on something and wanted to take a look, so we picked a place near a pub" – a reply which deceives no-one and isn't really meant to. So – never ever admit that you went aground by accident. You will, at least, have plenty of time to perfect your cover story.

Enough then of Breydon Water and Up the Junction. To be fair to the Broads, it isn't too bad – well – not as bad as all that. And, if you get by without making the spectators even lift an eyebrow, then Nelson (who, himself, left the Broads at a suspiciously early age) would have been proud of you.

There are many other Trog spectacles on tbe Broads which owe nothing to the rise and fall of the Yarmouth tides. The running battles between sailing yachts and motor cruisers, for instance. The yachts are, nine times out of ten, tacking back and forth in narrow rivers – 100 feet or so this way and then 100 feet or so the other – to gain, maybe, 20 feet in the desired direction. This fills the motor cruisers with a sense of one-upmanship because they can steer up the middle regardless. The sailing crews, however, have their own and permanent sense of one-upmanship because they are real sailors, aren't they and any one can steer a gin palace. With both sides feeling aggressive and with "steam gives way to sail" ever on the lips – the sailors play at last across the road in front of the cruisers, who, however, have the reprisal weapon of wash at their finger tips. By short tacks a yacht can hope to keep a cruiser at bay for a satisfying length of time, but, by bursts of wash, the cruiser can expect to dislodge any yacht crew who is silly enough to be standing up. The wash ploy can, it is true, be seen to best advantage at sea and in large harbours, but there is no lack of embryo talent on the Broads – which is a recognised Trog-Wash national training school for future drivers of floating gin-palaces. A good wash-man can expect to put at least two yachts aback and one aground in any given stretch of a mile and there is an unofficial, but well recognised score sheet which he can log:-

Dinghy capsized	1 point
Cooking meal removed from galley to cabin floor	2 points
Drinks capsized	½ point each drink
Crew capsized	2 points
Crew with drink capsized together	3 points
Yacht put aback	1 point
Yacht put aground	5 points
Crew put overboard	6 points
Helmsman overboard	10 points
Bank angler shakes fist	1 point
Yacht swamped and sunk	Game, set and match
Official launch incommoded in any way	Lose all previous score and run for life

Yachts are, for their part, not entirely helpless. Some are armed with duck-guns, all are armed with quants, and many are armed with bowsprits as well.

The bowsprit is that pointed bit of wood which sticks out from the sharp end like a sword-fish snout. It was invented many years ago by a Mr Denny Dessouter and is there for the ostensible purpose of allowing a foresail, or several foresails to be put further forward. In truth it is really part of Britain's maritime re-armament plan as anyone who has ever had someone else's bowsprit poked through his shrouds will know. On the Broads, bowsprits have been known to poke through the windows of bank-side bungalows and have skewered many an angler. Their main uses, however, are to protect the bows of the boat in run-of-the-mill collisions and to provide a fearsome ram in combat. Two bowspritted yachts having at each other, is a straight flash-back to Ivanhoe, Ashby de la Zouch, and knightly tourney. When two contestants manage to spear each other simultaneously through the rigging they cannot be prised apart save by the use of the emergency axe and hacksaw. Mostly, however, bowsprits are used against the common enemy, which is the motor cruiser, and the idea is to get the bowsprit through a cruiser cabin window. This is most easily done at night when the boats are tied up and are sitting ducks. Most of the day's feuds are settled – one way or another – at overnight resting places. Surreptitious casting adrift has been

known to take place – which, allied to the inevitable casting adrift which goes on from natural causes ("I gave it a full round turn and two half-hitches and it can't possibly have come undone") – produces the nightly confusion which is such a lovable part of a Broads' holiday. Half a dozen mixed boats, some inhabited, drifting gently and broadside down onto a low bridge *can* only eventually be sorted by an experienced log-jam man who can leap sure-footedly from craft to craft. There are few of these around, and by the attrition of occupational risk, there are fewer each season.

There is also always the danger of setting your own boat adrift unless you have taken careful stock of its name. The hire boats are all pretty much alike and the fact that when you went into the pub you had left yours in place A is no guarantee at all that it will still be in place A when you get back. Many a man has cast his dozing wife or girl friend adrift in the belief that he was getting his own back on that chap who luffed him up near Potter Heigham. Family explanations can then wear thin, especially if that blonde from the *Breydon Belle* happens to be on the landing stage at the time. Which reminds me that adroit use of the dumb-blonde ploy, should you have suitable material on board, can save a lot of rope work. It is surprising how much help from the shore the "I'm only a lost little girl" look can drum up. I once observed two such lasses – both of whom I knew to be quite competent – get the plum pub-side mooring, night after night, without dirtying their hands, by jumping ashore, ropeless, and striding out for the pub with the loud aside, "It'll be all right there Sue, I've left it in gear!"

Low bridges – like the one at Potter Heigham, can, of course, be great fun in their own right. Yachts have to take their masts down and drift, or quant, or motor through – which is all right if no-one stands up, or if the boat isn't sailing under its awning (which can happen if there is a reasonable wind and the awning is of fair size). Awnings and low bridges don't mix. Or rather they are apt to mix too much. It is, however, against motor cruisers that low bridges can really turn nasty. That pretty little stub mast on which you fly that splendid pennant you bought, which, at 20 yards, looks very like the RORC – that'll never see the first day out. One of the guide books says that if the driver of a motor cruiser puts his eye on the level of the top of the cabin roof and then gazes at the bridge, it is OK to press on if he can see the underside of the arch. Conversely, it is far from OK if he can't.

The truth of this is beyond dispute, but, equally beyond dispute, is that by the time the sight has been taken and fed into the computer, it is almost certainly too late. Reliance on this accounts for the presence at all bridges of quite a substantial "gate" of onlookers, many of whom have brought their picnic hampers, and others their grandchildren.

Come to think of it, there aren't too many places on the Broads which don't have their own permanent resident gallery. So, if you are suddenly aware of loneliness all around, you may well wonder if you haven't turned onto an un-navigable bit. One thing is for sure – you will soon find out. Another thing which is also for sure is that, having found out, no matter in how remote a place is your resultant agony, a gallery will appear, by magic, within ten minutes. It is the old Norfolk motto again – never let a happening go unwatched and, with any luck, there might even be money in it.

5

Canals

I have never myself been afloat on a canal west of Suez. I have several times been afloat *in* one, because as a small boy I used to fish and fall in whatever canal it is that wanders around the Rugby-Coventry-Stratford-Banbury-Oxford lump of my native countryside. There was then no pleasure-boating, or none that I saw, but a lot of commercial barges. I recall that they were all wonderfully decorated in many colours and that fat women in black were perpetually dunking flower-painted buckets over the side and pulling up pails full of the slimy green water and sloshing the contents around with mops. They were very efficient at capturing a full bucket's worth every time, which they did by banging the open top of the bucket down with force and elan into the water more or less vertically. I must have stored away the secret of this action somewhere in my tiny mind, because when, in full time, I found myself having to haul water for washing down boat decks, it was every throw a coconut. And, if I am paying attention – it still is so today. A minor art, but a satisfying one.

The barges of my day were still over 90 per cent horse-drawn and those with chuffy motors were considered upstart – not only among the bargees themselves, but by us small boys on the bank. We were very partisan on the matter, though for what reason escapes me. Perhaps we are, indeed, all born as little Conservatives.

My only other truck with barges was in a houseboat conversion of one on the river Soar near Leicester. A friend and his wife lived in it, and very roomy and comfortable it was. It had an engine and one day we actually started it and moved the barge all of two miles for a picnic, of which I still retain some faded photographs. Later, this barge – or monkey-boat, as its owner called it – or narrow boat, as I believe it would now be known, was sunk in a gale at its moorings. It has never been clear to me why. The owners were away on holiday and we all had to buckle to and rescue it and dry everything out before their return – which we did. And, with this, ended my happily fleeting personal contact with barges and canals.

That there is now a revival of canal use, no reader of the Practical Boat Owner can be ignorant of. There are in it pages of splendid maps showing that you can barge or cruise all over England, if you know which forks to take. The telly, too, constantly shows us bands of devotees shifting mud or clearing out old bicycles to open up yet another stretch of some unsalubrious inland waterway. I must admit it leaves me cold to know that one can now wander round the back slums of Birmingham in a boat, because, for me, the assumption that a back slum of Birmingham is, per se, attractive from any angle is not valid. None the less there are people a plenty who like cruising the canals and who own or hire suitable craft in which to do it. There are even marinas. A good friend of mine goes "cutting" every year, and since she is a born and competitive sea-type sailor and wins cups in dinghies in force 6 in the Channel, there must be an attraction. Perhaps it's the change. She says it's the cows, of which there are so few between Hayling Island and Bembridge Ledge. She also maintains that I am wasting my time mentioning canal cruising in a Trog book because there are no Trogs on the canals – period.

This, I do not believe. There are, for example, great mountain-climbing stairs of locks on canals and, I believe, each user operates these locks for himself with a boy's do-it-yourself flood-the-county kit which comes with the boat. The Trog-potential of such stairways of locks, with a combined rise which would take you up the side of Ben Nevis, must be being exploited by someone. I hope so.

There is one major fact to which canal sailors can proudly point – Hornblower himself once commanded a canal barge. As I recall – and without bothering to look it up – he was in a hurry to get from the Midlands (what the dickens was he doing in the Midlands?) back to the Admiralty to go off to win Aboukir Bay or Copenhagen, and he took passage in a barge.* Inevitably he soon was in charge of it and "legged" it through some tunnels before a triumphant arrival at, I suppose, Regents Park, Little Venice, or St John's Wood tube station.

** I remember now – he was going to London to take charge of Nelson's funeral.*

But, being a fair minded chap – I'll leave my barge-toting friend and part-time foredeck crew to add a final word or two if only to preserve, as the BBC says, the balance of the programme.

No, I didn't say there aren't any Canal Trogs, but, unlike River Trogs, Water Ski-ing Trogs, Sea Trogs and the Author, they are generally more of a menace to themselves than to others and are, therefore, by my definition, not really True Trogs at all.

On the subject of tunnels, these are not only dark, but are full of dripping water, swelling here and there into minor waterfalls. It being basically impossible to steer a narrow boat from inside, the helmsman is apt to get exceedingly wet when negotiating a tunnel, quite apart from the discovery that the rest of the crew have retreated to the cabin, in a cowardly way, and refuse to come out to discuss or enjoy the passing beauties of nature, such as limestone stratification and the varieties of moss picked out by the headlight.

As I said, tunnels are one of the reasons why there are few Trogs on the canals and their scarcity may account for the fact that the full potential for disaster on the cuts has not yet been realised.

On the other hand, the Trog who comes to the canals from an apprenticeship on the Thames, will find some interesting variations. To start with, a canal is not actually flowing. Apart from discovering that potato peelings thrown overboard are still there next morning, this lack of flow produces interesting effects at locks. The Trog who has learnt, when below a large Thames lock, that when sluices ("paddles" to the real "cutter") are opened, the water flows "downhill" rather faster, is due for a surprise. The narrowness of most canals and the siting of the paddles frequently results in a sudden surge and gurgle of water "uphill" when the paddles are open. Our Trog, neatly tied up by a piece of string from the sharp end, will find himself either rushing forward, if the string is a long one, until he rams the lock gate very smartly, or if the string is too short, the back-end swings out until the whole thing is firmly wedged across the entrance. If the first manoeuvre is done properly, preferably with a narrow boat, and the lock is hit hard enough, it may even open the gate sufficiently to allow a violent spurt of water to escape, which, with skill, can be made to go straight through the open front door of the cabin. There it may help to revive the crew who will have been knocked prostrate on the floor by the original crunch. A second variation on this theme is better done with the plastic bath-tub type of cruiser, which is usually sharp enough to get properly wedged in the lock doors. Assuming, however, that our Trog manages to get into the lock, there is more scope for spectator enjoyment, as most locks are a nominal 7 ft wide, while most canal boats are an equally nominal 6ft. 10ins. A snug fit, you may think, but as the locks tend to taper towards the top, the fit can get even snugger. A high floating plastic cruiser, with fenders dangling, is then interesting to watch as the water starts to rise. This pushes his fenders upwards to the rubbing strake and, with any luck, the onlooker who has chosen his lock wisely, will be rewarded by the sight of a real Trog jam. The water will go on rising even when the boat – now jammed by its fenders in the tapering lock – has ceased to respond. As the water comes over the captive gunwhales, the frenzied crew will be rushing up and down the lock side fighting over the operating handle and arguing whether to stop letting it in at the top, or to start letting it out at the bottom. With any luck they may settle this issue by dropping the handle into the lock.

I have now given my all on the subject of canals and of Troggery on same. When one thinks that a well placed barge can probably reach across from bank to bank, and so effectively stop all inland waterway navigation in either direction in its area, I just don't believe that this feat isn't regularly achieved. When one also thinks of the opportunities vouchsafed to motor-propelled hired barges to slither down a precipice of lock stairs on the crest of a cleverly contrived waterfall – I, equally, don't believe that this chance is left a-begging. In fact – with Hilaire Belloc – I find it difficult to believe that the whole of the southern Midlands isn't permanently under water.

6

Home is the Sailor (and dressed for the part)

So we come to that Mecca of all Trogs Afloat – to the ultimate scene, to the place where it all happens – to the nation's heritage – the sea.

All else is make-believe. The Captain of a gin palace on the Thames, for all his reefer jacket, brass buttons and white topped cap, is fooling nobody. He may be wearing the full Arsenal gear, but he is playing fourth division football. To make my point – now and then there strays into the upper-Thames, an obvious sea-goer – sail or power – to king it like a lion among zebra. Its very aura of the wild blue yonder lays bare the pretentions of all the natty river yachts. In fairness, I must add that no-one is more aware of this than its crew and they love it. Their salty jeans, thick off-white sweaters and bare feet are a studied contrast to the seldom-quite-right suburban boating attire of the lesser mortals. The glimpse of yellow oilskins in the cabin rubs it in that these are people from another and more romantic world.

The pub table conversation of these visiting gods is, as you would require, modest and quiet, but – again I must admit – not so quiet that those nearby cannot hear snatches of "force six on the nose", and so-casual mention of buoys and beacons of far sounding names. There is little doubt that they are enjoying the glamour they have brought to the banks of Staines, and that they know the bourgeoisie is being duly épatered. Sometimes, though, I have just wondered what a 30 foot bilge keel sloop, with its mast unstepped and its diesel put-putting, is doing of a summer's day, hanging about Runnymede.

Let us, however, not tarry with them, but hasten to whence they came – or whence they appear to have come – the genuine and boundless sea, guaranteed the same as sailed by Drake, Frobisher, Nelson, Hornblower, Bolitho, both the Hawkinses, Mr Onedin, Sir Francis Chichester, Sir Alec Rose and Robin Knox Johnston.

The first prerequisite of sailing the sea is a harbour. This means a bit of the ocean which is protected or sheltered in some way by stone walls, breakwaters, or by enfolding land – and inside which boats can, more or less, safely graze. Most harbours are in river estuaries of some kind so that its channel has been provided by thousands of years of eroding nature taking its course and manufacturing its mud. Or they are on inlets where the sea has flooded and carved its way inland until – all passion spent – it has dwindled into marsh and saltings.

The south-east coast and the south coast, happily, abound in such, and as they mainly have no golden sands, only grey-black goo, and as they have no slot machines or bingo, civilisation has passed them by. This means that you can usually get there without fighting too many Trog actions on the roads – the Trog Troops being more deployed defensively around the promenade resorts which are on your actual coastline and not, thank God, up muddy creeks and estuaries.

Once at a harbour you are free to observe the Trog and non-Trog life with which the boats and quays and jetties are beset.

The first and major point of differentiation is dress, and for the notebooks, I give you this basic guide to which the student can add his own observations almost ad infinitum.

Non-Trog – Male

Head-gear
Woolly hats with or without bobbles.

Student-type peaked caps – usually blue and unadorned, worn à la Princess Anne.

White topped naval type caps, providing they are off-white, old, badgeless or only discreetly badged. A genuine Royal Navy Petty Officer's cap is acceptable if worn by someone who was clearly (or maybe still is) at least a Rear Admiral.

Oilskin hats, like in the old cod liver oil ads – but only when raining and in dinghy or afloat.

Neckwear
Never – save on shore at formal club dinners, when yachting ties with white collar are permissible to senior citizens and club officers, and those hoping to be elected next year.

Torso-gear
Naked torso.

Any old shirt – preferably torn and paint covered.

Sweaters – whether on their own or over a shirt. The sweater must be thick, old and dirty, but can be any colour. Old cricket sweaters will do, but only of the best clubs.

T shirts – just.

Nether-gear
Bathing trunks

Shorts.

Jeans

Any old (R) old lightweight trousers.

So-called "Breton" trousers – usually red – preferably torn and daubed with anti-fouling paint.

Socks
Never – well, hardly ever.

Footwear
None

Deck-shoes

Sandals

Sea-boots of any kind, from "anklet" ones up to full thigh.

Jackets
Double-breasted blue reefer, or dark blue blazer – and only at guest nights ashore.

Buttons – black with club insignia just visible.

Brass – well-er-maybe.

Over-Jackets
Oilskins or similar deck-gear, or an off the shoulder blanket.

NB. trousers – if not self-sustaining, may be tied by rope or string, or by a lanyard with or without knife.

Non-Trog – Female

Pretty well as above except for the naked torso bit.

Headscarves are permissible.

Ashore, pressed slacks, sweaters, small nautical or club brooch, deck shoes or sandals, caps.

Trog – (either sex)

White flannels or ducks

Braces

Footwear with heels

Rex Harrison cardigans

Dresses

Jewellery, except maybe bracelet or brooch aforementioned

Almost anything male that looks smart

Almost anything feminine that looks feminine (except your actual female)

Bikinis – especially bikinis

Nautical caps with big gold club badges. (I have one and my crew won't let me wear it).

White topped caps with "Putney Garage" stamped inside.

Sweaters or T shirts with boat names on them, other than proper boat names like "Morning Cloud", or "Prospect of Whitby", or "Adventurer". A sweater or anorak emblazoned "Rover of Emsworth" – No. (If there is a real "Rover of Emsworth" – I am truly sorry).

All clothing that looks deliberately or aggressively or overcooked 'nautical'. Anyone who has ever been on a French golf course and seen the clothes the French wear *pour le golf,* in the odd belief that those are the sort of clothes the hated English wear for playing proper golf in, will take the point.

A note on accessories. Stop watches hung on lanyards round necks are OK – so are big wrist watches with knobs springing out all round. These are the tools which enable dinghy racers to win without actually being caught cheating – or to heighten their chances of not being rumbled. Gear may be carried about in duffle bags and old canvas bags of any kind and also grocers' boxes – but never in a suitcase (they don't stow, see).

Female crew are allowed handbags providing they are of the airline bag type – preferable with a yacht club insignia woven into the side, which means they cost a bomb. This may also mean that the female or her escort is actually a member of the club, but this is not essential unless the club be the Royal Yacht Squadron, when it is advisable to join first. In any event, they don't allow women members – or certainly didn't when they turned Queen Victoria down. This un-amused her so much that she wouldn't let Albert belong either, and founded the Royal Victoria at Ryde as her revenge – or so they do say.

Professional clothing and gear is another thing altogether. Those who make their living on and around the sea, like fishermen and ferrymen and boatyard people, can and do wear anything they damn well choose – cloth caps and braces included. There is never any doubt that they "belong" and their gear is for real comfort and utility and in no way modulated by any desire to impress. Which is more than the rest of us can say.

7

Over the Harbour Wall

The student is now in a position to make a rough quayside Trog-identification by the application of the simple clothing and gear tests just outlined.

There is, however, much more to it than that. Troggery is not just clobber-deep. There are plenty of other dead give-aways which can be quietly observed from the relaxing comfort of the harbour wall. For non-boating types on holiday the spotting and recording of these clues could well be the basis of a pencil and paper game as they take their ease in the sun. A lot, for example, revolves about dinghies or tenders, the arrival and departure and tying up of same, and above all, the methods of boarding and disembarking. All these feats are on free public and entertaining display at any quayside.

Most dinghies, which are used as tenders back and forth from the shore to moored yachts or other larger boats, anchored, parked, or otherwise secured some way out, are of the rubber or blow-up variety. Some are of wood or plastic. All have oars, and some a small outboard as well. The inflatables will usually have the name of the mother-ship painted or daubed on the stern preceded by "Tender to..." or, more often, just "T.T." – as in "T.T. Sea Rover" plus, maybe, the port – like "Poole", or a yacht or sailing club like "Mudflat S.C.". The wordage will, you can bet, usually be a minimum, because painting a line of letters is not something many people can do very well – even with stencils, while painting letters on rubber is yet another art in itself. Ready-bought stick-on letters tend not to – especially weak-structure letters like "M". My own inflatable has long been identified just as " oonfleet. Bosha ".

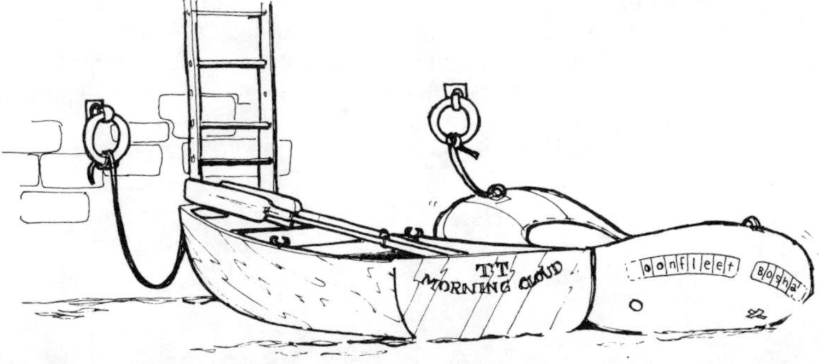

There are several objectives in putting this writing on a dinghy. The first and most important is to establish to the onlooker that you are the owner of a real live yacht "out there" and the little dinghy you happen to be in at the moment is merely a means of reaching it. For that reason you hardly see a dinghy which hasn't got "Tender to" or "T.T." on it – whether the occupant has actually got a yacht or no. Other, and purely minor, reasons are to identify the dinghy after a good dinner ashore, or so that it can be traced back to you when it goes adrift, either from the quayside or from once having been in tow behind your main boat.

There is a bit of one-upmanship about Yacht Club initials painted on tenders. Most owners who happen to belong to a club with an "R" for "Royal" in it, can't resist it – and the demi-gods who can paint simply "R.Y.S." seldom even try. Some owners add a transferred club insignia on the bows, but this is a bit much and can be marked up as "Trog". Borderline Trog are the highly polished wooden tenders with carved decor at the stern and very expensive coloured insignia plaques either side of the bow. When such tenders are propelled by a hired hand in uniform and the name of the boat across his jersey, it borders on vulgar ostentation and is so envied by one and all that they are reduced, as I am, to open sneering. It will, of course, either belong to a Peer of the Realm, a full Admiral of the Fleet, or more probably, to a former rating who got into the scrap iron business after the war.

There is, then, much simple fun to be had by merely observing the dinghies as such. There is even more fun in watching them come alongside to tie up.

The old hand will tend to do one of two things. He will, if it is low tide, and if the depth of water allows, row or motor up, bows-on to the shallows, off the end of a hard (often a pebble-bestrewn path through the mud) and jump into the shallows over the sharp end, the dinghy rope or painter in hand. Or, if there is water up to your actual quayside, he may come up alongside a ladder.

If the former – observe his feet. If naked, then either he is a really tough old salt, or maybe he is a masochist. If he has sea-boots or sandals on, then there is no problem, but, if he (or more often his lady passenger) is already shod for the shore or even wearing socks, then the chances are recriminations will break out. This will end up in the male taking off his shoes, hanging them round his neck, rolling up his trousers, and paddling a yard or so to pull the dinghy up with female grimly in the back until she can step out onto the hard like a lady. Mark them down as Trogs. If he of the naked feet marches unflinchingly up the pebbles, dragging his dinghy ashore after him, give him homage. If he hops about in agony – mark him down as an exhibitionist.

And now to our ladder-lander. Here your observations should focus on how he gets onto the ladder – how he climbs it – if he remembers the dinghy painter (rope), and how he ties it up.

If, having stowed his oars, he stands confidently up in the dinghy and then leaps for the nearest rung -- its 6 to 4 on he'll go into the drink. Either the dinghy will shoot sharpish away as he uses it as a springboard, and he'll go flat on his face in the water – or, if he makes the ladder, he'll slide down it. If, however, he hangs on tight to the ladder with one hand and pulls himself upright, and then, still holding on, climbs firmly out, bringing the painter with him – then there'll be no free entertainment out of him. Now and then an athletic young man will leap grandly from his still moving dinghy onto the ladder – painter in hand – and make it in one flowing movement. Keep your eye out for him next time. Sooner or later he'll catch his foot in the painter and it will all go gloriously wrong. With luck you may be there to enjoy it.

It should be noted that a very high percentage – up in the 90s – of boat people who fall into the 'oggin', do so when getting into or out of dinghies. The laws of average are well on your side in this particular spectator sport.

Once ashore – wet or dry – note next how and where the dinghy is tied up. If, by a quick smooth hitch, followed by a security-testing tug and not a glance backward as he strides away, the chap has done it before. But if, by a studied piece of knotmanship by someone who is clearly trying to remember the diagram in the scouts' manual, then you may expect to see the dinghy go adrift fairly soon. A very painstaking repetition of the same hitch, however, followed by an extra knot or two "to make sure", means that the fun will start when the chap comes back and wants to untie it all. If you have a pocket knife, keep it handy. He may not have one of his own.

Perhaps of more significance than the manner of tying-up is the "where". The extreme case comes from the man who drags the dinghy a couple of yards above the water line and leaves it there on a flooding tide while he goes for a quick one. He is never quick enough. A usual case is that of adding a painter to a little collection already hitched invitingly round a ring or rung a little way up a wall. This is probably psychologically motivated by a desire to avoid being the odd man out or as an expression of inner insecurity. Either way, ten minutes later the other dinghy owners return, unhitch, and depart, leaving our friend's tender all alone in its glory to be swamped.

Knowledge of the state of the local tide greatly enhances your pleasurable anticipation of happenings with dinghies. Often there is a notice board somewhere around the harbour which conveys this information. If not – a glance at the moored yachts will tell you. (If they are lying bows towards where the tide comes from, then it is flooding – and vice versa). Take your check on this from sailing yachts which have keels, not motor boats or small craft which haven't, as they will often be lying to the wind more than the tide.

Talking of wind and tide reminds me that, in their own right, these add much to the gaiety of the scene. Both factors affect dinghies about equally, which becomes apparent when they are being eased up to a quay wall. We have already seen what can happen on the gentle Thames when a boat tries to tie up the wrong end first. In the sea – with maybe a two knot tide and a 15 knot wind, plus some actual waves, the affair can get as speeded up as an old Buster Keaton movie – and with a matching entertainment value.

The average tender-load consists of Dad (at the oars) and Mum at the blunt end moaning ceaselessly because the water keeps breaking equally over the stern of the boat and the stern of Mum (always wear oilskin trousers in a choppy sea). The sharp end of the dinghy will be given over to empty water containers – toilet bags – a plastic bag full of gash and, maybe, a soggy carton of something. Dad is looking over his shoulder every other stroke so he can see where he's going. Incidentally, I have only ever met one captain who has got this dinghy business really sorted. He sits proudly (and sensibly protected) in the stern-sheets wearing his club cap and, from time to time, pointing majestically shorewards, or acknowledging respectful salutes from the trot of yachts as he passes. One charming young lady is at the oars and another is crouched in the bows ready to leap splashily into the shallows and drag the dinghy in. Master can then walk ashore while delicate hands hold the dinghy steady for his dignified and dry exit. This he makes with never a downward glance as the girls get busy making the tender fast and humping the gear. He tells me that he trained them with the help of a whip, but that now he finds that unnecessary, and, "I just buy them gin instead". On one trip I borrowed one of these splendid Girl Fridays for my boat. When it came dinghy time I hurriedly put on my Trog cap and sat at the blunt end. Girl Friday appeared with three duffle bags, handed them in, and then sat beside me. She only spoke three words – "Get to rowing", she said..... not even "Sir!".

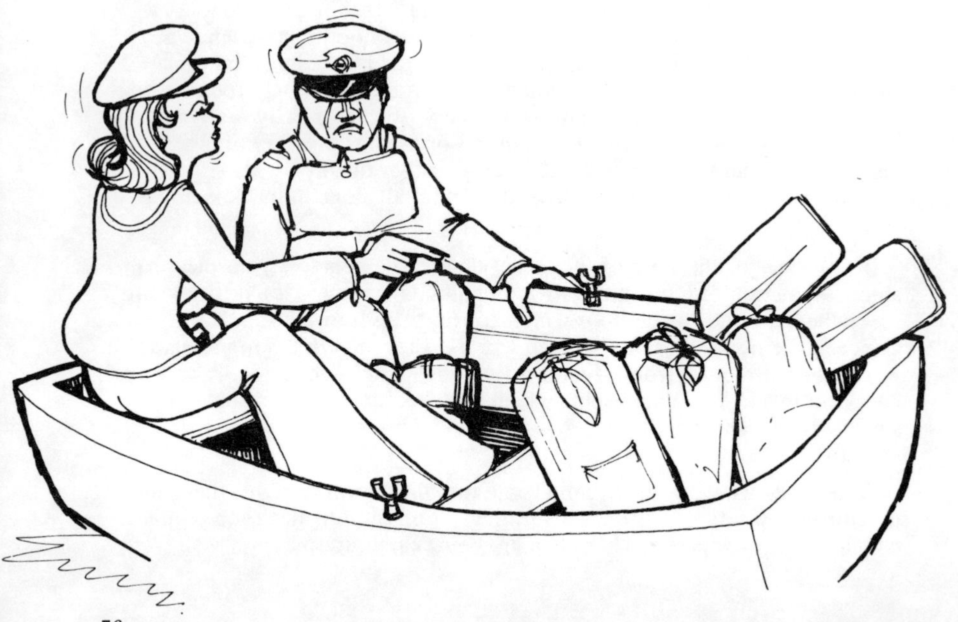

To return to Dad and Mum and all the gear in the storm tossed dinghy. Dad says it will be easier to row up the slope of the slipway. Mum says maybe, but when the bows touch, the waves will then really break over the blunt end (which they will) and may she remind Dad just who is at the blunt end and it isn't him. Dad then says they'll go alongside that far ladder, and Mum says no, because she can only reach the bottom rung and the bottom rung is covered with wet mud. The first ladder is better. Dad says that the water's rougher there – by which time he is abreast of it heading down tide. He tries to grab a rung – half ships the landward oar, which is sticking out and getting in the way, misses and the oar falls into the water. Have you ever tried to manoeuvre a dinghy in a tideway with one oar? It is wholly beyond Dad, who spins round in circles – still going down tide. Mum finally grabs the mud covered second ladder as it passes – rescues the oar, woman-hauls the dinghy round bows to tide and says now she's got mud all over her – which she has. Mum goes up the ladder first and Dad hands her the painter which she ties with a grocer's knot. Dad hands her up all the gear, which Mum plonks onto the quayside with protest in every plonk, after which she stalks off in a screaming silence. Sympathetic hands help Dad onto the quay – they've all been there themselves. "It's part of the fun, old boy", they say – and, do you know, for a flick of a moment, they even believe it. Meanwhile I keep buying gin for the two Girl Fridays – you never know your luck!

Getting into the dinghy is, however, more noteworthy than getting out, and will repay a Trog spotter's major study. The basic trick is to avoid giving the dinghy any form of outward propulsion with your foot at the moment when you commit yourself to follow that leading foot with yourself. No-one has ever successfully boarded a receding dinghy – or, if they have, I've never seen them. I have, however, seen plenty of spectacular failures and have even tried it a couple of times myself. On one memorable occasion my wife and I tried it simultaneously – though I must make the point that it was a dark night and we had dined rather well. Now we jump boldly – but not at the same time – for the far side.

So – for the notebook:

Trog
Going down a ladder – face outwards.

Getting feet in the dinghy while the boarder's centre of gravity is still outboard of it, unless supported by firm grip on the shore.

Putting weight on near side of dinghy.

Getting into dinghy successfully with painter still tied up out of reach.

Non Trog
The reciprocal of the above.

Sooner or later the student will see a real pro get into his dinghy. If it is fully afloat he will leap cleanly in and land without a totter, or without setting up as much as a single rock-a-by. If it is just pulled up, bows lightly ashore and astern afloat, he will still jump in, but in such a way that his impetus will launch it at the same time. It is most impressive and is way beyond the ability of any Trog.

"It is by their dinghy work that you shall know them" – and that, too, can be done in poker work and hung up in the cabin.

8

"Out There"

For the ensuing Trog actions and recognition features, the student has no alternative but to take to sea himself. It is the only way he can make the necessary observations. Preferably he should do this in a well manned commercial boat plying for hire and reward, with not less than two engines, plus a steadying sail and in a wind force not greater than the standard Solent weekend gale-rating of Force 3 (take a reef at Force 3½ and, above Force 4, stay on your mooring and open the medicinal gin).

We have already said enough – well, enough to whet the appetite – about the excitements of dinghy work, so we will assume that our Trog Mum and Dad have managed to clamber on board their yacht unhurt, which I may say, is one hell of an assumption. Boarding ladders are rickety things – dinghies are bouncy ones, yachts have steep sides and, out on the deep-water moorings, there are always either real waves or wash-waves from passing craft. Which is why so many Trogs are to be found huddled in Marinas where they can step aboard from floating platforms owned by millionaires, or by people who are just about to become millionaires. I will not dwell on Marinas at this moment because I aim to spread myself on the subject later.

However, with our Trog crew safely and gratefully on board their 22 foot, 4 berth, bilge keel, family sloop, they are now busy preparing for the week-end adventure of actually leaving the mooring and going somewhere. The whereabouts of the "somewhere" has already been the subject of some debate. The shipping forecast has spoken of a southerly wind, Force 2/3 for Wight, which Dad reckons is splendid for going to Cowes (15 miles) and about which Mum is suspicious because Force 5 was also mentioned in the forecast – albeit for Iceland ("It might be all right today, but what about coming back tomorrow?"). Mum, in fact, really wants to stay inside Chichester Harbour and is actively distrustful of what she calls "Out There" – which means all seas and oceans south of Hayling Island or, at worst, south, east and west of West Pole buoy. Dad is equally determined to go to Cowes so that he can make casual, but continual reference to the fact at the office on Monday. His main worry is that the Force 2/3 is probably true for south of the Island, but in its lee, in the Solent, it will probably be only Force ½, and he isn't so sure if his engine will cope for 10 windless miles out of the 15. Further – Mum is well known not to like the engine running because it is noisy and rattles and fills the cabin with smells.

Dad is buttoning on the big genoa foresail to the forestay and Mum (who is against all genoas in principle) is banging the cups about preparatory to making coffee as soon as the boat is under way. She knows they are going to Cowes and is only intent on building up Dad's back-log of debt to the little woman so that he will stump up for a night in the Marina when they get there. This will mean a walk-off-walk-on facility and no clambering into and out of the dinghy. It could also, if she plays her cards right, mean a meal out instead of cooking one in the galley, and if the dreaded Force 5 does come, then she will see to it they go home on the ferry. Mum begins to brighten up.

Dad now has the mainsail hoisted as well as the genoa – both free and flapping mildly in the local Force 1½ – and he has the engine started – just in case. The tide is on the last hour and a half of the flood, and Dad reckons he should clear Chichester Harbour bar just in time to pick up the west-going ebb which will, with luck, last all the 15 miles to Cowes and carry him there – wind or no wind. If it doesn't – with his 2'6" of draft – he can always duck into Wooton Creek – albeit at low tide.

What, however, is currently worrying Dad is that weekly moment of truth – actually getting started. He has lines of boats ahead of him and other such lines astern – with two moored motor boats off to either side. If he sails off, then the flood may well take him backwards in such light airs and into his next astern. But, if he motors off, he will lose face because Nelson never had an engine. True, but like I have said before, Nelson didn't only have a crew of one Mum whose attitude to the whole voyage was on the minus side of neutral. So Dad decides to motor-off – and bully for Dad. No Trog marks should be awarded against him for this because he couldn't possibly make south down his home creek under sail anyway. It is dead into wind and tide, and short tacks wouldn't gain him a yard, apart from making him lose the first of the ebb "out there". So he bravely calls for Mum to cast off the buoy and nudges the boat up on engine to take off its weight on the mooring chain while she does so.

This is the moment where the day can be made or marred. If the mooring chain and its rope tail and the buoy are all robbled round the forward cleat for Mum to unravel, and if Dad has so put up the foresail that it stops the buoy going out over the sharp end – there really is going to be a sharp interchange of domestic chat and certainly no coffee.

Dad – whose true Troggery is beginning to be open to some doubt – has, in fact, already tidied up the buoy and chain situation, so all that Mum has to do is to unhitch one turn and chuck the lot overboard. Which she duly does. Dad goes into forward gear and chugs down the channel, gathering in the free yardage of jib and main sheets while keeping his prop clear of his own mooring rope. At the end of his own channel he turns 90 to starboard and is now beam on to the breeze. He pays out both his sails to the right (port tack) and motor-sails happily at 4½ knots on a broad reach over the dying flood and towards East Head – Hayling Island and the Call of the Open Sea. Mum makes some coffee and all's well with the world. And so it continues to be until there is this dinghy race off Hayling. Dad is making tacks close-hauled to the southerly breeze, towards West Pole, and still has half a mile of southing to do before he can pay off onto his westward reach – hopefully for the rest of the day. The tide is about high, with deceitful water over the Winner Sands on his left, and if he sticks on them he'll be there for 12 hours unless he can get a quick kick off. The echo-sounder is on, but the engine is off, for domestic reasons. Then, from astern, comes an attack by the best part of 100 dinghies, all with their racing burgees up and ripping about all round. Mum says she'd rather not watch and goes below. Dad is edging too close to the Winners, and wants to turn right onto the port tack before he goes aground. If he does so he will cut across the bows of half a dozen dinghies overhauling him, and, if he holds on for them to go by, there are still dozens more where they came from. A cruising boat must give way to a racing one and, if he turns, he'll be on port and they'll be on starboard, so they will have a double right of way. Poor old Dad. He does the only thing he can. He luffs up dead into the wind and comes to a flapping halt, and starts his engine to edge away to deeper water. Dinghies shoot about all round him and maybe one crew in one dinghy acknowledges with a flip of the hand that Dad has done them proud. Some Trog marks, however, could well be handed out to the racing boys. They have their competitive problems, but the cruising boats in a narrow channel have theirs as well. They are nothing like so handy or so fast as a racing dinghy which, if it touches the sand, can raise its centre board an inch clear and spin round on the opposite tack in a second.

I remember once tacking painfully up a narrow channel, fighting the ebb with no engine (out of fuel) and losing half an hour's worth of territorial gain because a Fireball – not even racing – came skimming over the shallows at high speed at my bows shouting "starboard" and forcing me to luff to avoid a collision. He did it again ten minutes later. This time I took no notice and he made such a violent last minute alteration of protest that he capsized and I was ever so glad and said so.

But, eventually, the dinghy swarm leaves Dad alone and deploys itself all round other victims – rather like fire ships buzzing about the Armada. I have long believed that if Glenda Jackson's Old Sea Dogs had had a couple of Solent trained dinghy squadrons with a boxful of flares each, none of the Spaniards would ever have made it past the Needles.

However, Dad has survived to turn due west at West Pole and sets off, broad reached and happy, for the Forts, which he can see, and no problem of navigation rears its ugly head. The "Hotels Conspic" west of the cultural centre of Hayling, can be seen on the Hampshire shore and if the set-in towards Langstone puts Dad to the north of the old Forts off Portsmouth, he can always say he was going through that flaming barrier which runs from north Fort to the land, via the Dolphins gap instead. Mum has just come up into the cockpit with drinks when the first fully paid up Trog of the day comes by at 20 knots, and at ten yards distance, in his tycoon-model Gin Palace. The wash puts the boat on one ear and then the other, and sends Mum crashing into the side of the cockpit and the drinks crashing into the sea. Dad – failing to cling to the tiller – is also shot to one side and then back again and finishes with Mum on the floor. A teenage starlet in a bikini, lying on the after deck of the Gin Palace, waves a languid hand as if she is doing a TV commercial for Holidays Afloat and, as Dad gets up to grab for the tiller, the boat gybes – the boom comes over and just misses his head by half an inch.

It's not that all Gin Palace drivers are Trogs – that would be an unsupportable allegation. It's just the odd 99 per cent of them that are the trouble. To define a Gin Palace:- it is a motor powered device – usually upwards of 30 ft long (maybe a 100 ft) – with a wheelhouse, and a big foredeck littered with assorted Trog women in dark glasses and little else. It is flying a lot of flags in all the wrong places, and is driven by a middle-aged and usually stoutish man sitting on a helmsman's chair behind a chromium wheel and lots of dashboard dials. You can bet your life he'll be wearing all the gear in the book and have a white top on his yachting cap and be drinking gin. He will already have capsized half a dozen dinghies that morning and, before he gets to Poole (the home harbour of so many such Palaces) he will have turned over half a dozen more. He will also have notched a few badly bruised ribs aboard sailing cruisers and, on a good day, maybe even a broken one, plus one or two unwary crew washed overboard.

The device with which he attacks all shipping in sight – at least all that is smaller than he is – will have cost anything from £10,000 to £100,000 and will be registered in the name of some company, or chain of garages or other, and be charged to tax. As far as I know there is nothing one can do about this breed of Trog. It's no good shaking your fist, because by the time you've picked yourself up, he's way and gone and is shooting up close alongside his next target. I suppose you could report him to his yacht club – if you could read it, and if he's got a yacht club. Or you might sue him for damages and grievous bodily harm. Or write to the Times.

Back on the farm – Mum has picked herself up and is really badly bruised and says so. Dad has regained control and is cursing all Gin Palace Trogs and also himself for allowing the Palace to jump him from astern. With a better look out, he could have shouted a warning to Mum to "hold on". Mum has already made this point once or twice.

So – with a special Trog identification note in your book, we continue – Westward Ho for Cowes – (or maybe Wooton Creek).

The next anti-Dad combined Trog offensive comes out of Portsmouth/Gosport when he is busy dodging battleship buoys, wreck buoys and the Royal Navy's Mining Ground (does it really have mines in it?), having safely passed through the chop which dwells around the Forts. The attack comes from a horde of outboard-motorised skimming dishes, tempted out by a calm sea and the light winds to the lee of the Island. Dad, who is a great upholder of the freedom of the National Heritage, is often of an illiberal mind to insert one exclusion clause which would read, "Except for Speedboats and Gin Palaces". He believes speedboats to be unsafe, noisy and, by and large, inconsiderately driven. It is not that they make all that much wash when planing, but that they are basically of hostile intent, and they frighten him stiff. Each skimming dish is the expensive pride and joy of some young chap who is cutting a dash with some young girl who, in turn, thinks she has stepped into the world of the Martini commercials. The skimming dishes are, in fact, the sex-wagons of the sea, and Dad's lumbering crate, flapping on the ebb, is just the thing for them to beat-up. Dad may think of himself as Hornblower every time he crosses Spithead, but every one of these chaps is Peter Scott chasing German MTB's on the Dover Patrol, and Dad just has to learn to put up with it. They don't actually hit him, but they do force Dad to start his engine so that he can have a bit of manoeuvre in reserve in case one of them makes a mess of it, or hits a waterlogged lump of driftwood, or just plain loses the place – which, one day, one of them is bound to. So he motors in a nil wind until the enemy horde is scattered by a pincer movement from the Ryde Hovercraft and the Ryde ferry, which latter could stand direct hits from a dozen speedboats and is conducted accordingly.

This, incidentally, is no place to keep reciting to oneself the old and often unreasonable maxim law of the sea about power giving way to sail. Enormous tankers coming into and out of Fawley, and liners and freighters and car ferries from and to Southampton, have enough to bother about to keep in their deep water channels without playing hide and seek with a thousand Solent yachts. Compared to a tanker, even Dad's family cruiser can spin on a sixpence, whereas the tanker couldn't stop in less than several miles, even if it wanted to. It has no brakes and precious little steering ability without endangering the whole ship. So, out with the notebooks and write large that old, old saying about being right dead right as he sailed along. Only Trogs of the truest blue hold course across the bows of Esso Nell because right is on his side.

When in the shipping lanes, and especially the main English Channel shipping lanes, there is only one set of assumptions a Trog Captain can safely make. These are:-

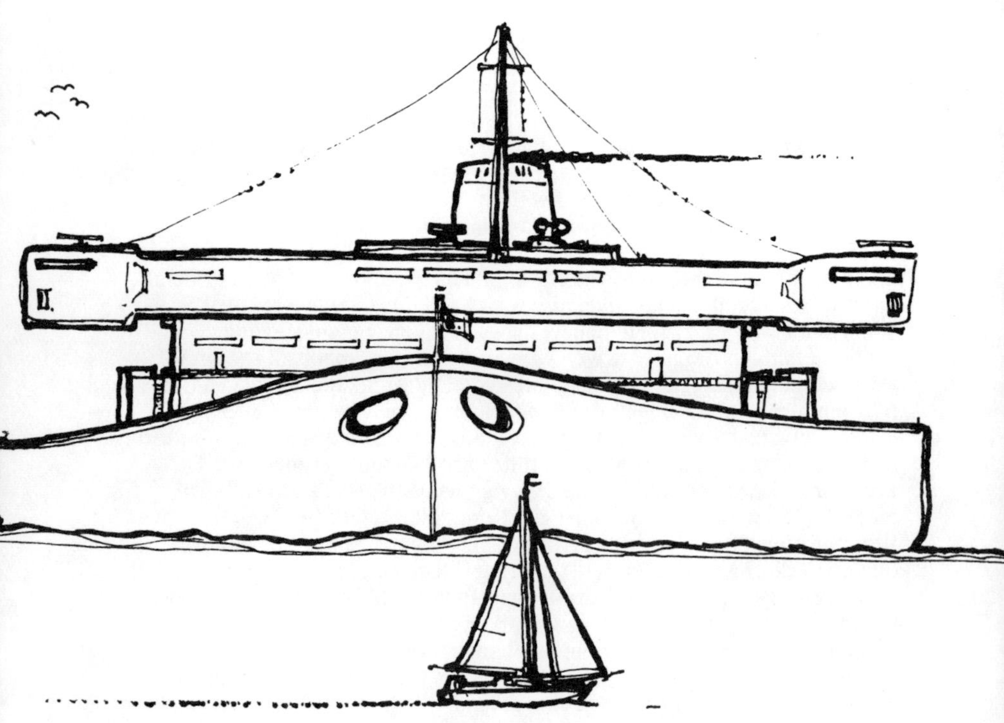

i All big ships are foreigners and lack the seamanship and discipline of the Master-Mariner race to which it is not their fault they have the misfortune not to belong.

ii There is, therefore, no watchkeeper on the bridge, or if there is, he is, he is either asleep or blinded by Gaulloise smoke. The ship will probably have been built in Japan, be flying the Liberian flag, be owned in America and skippered by a Greek.

iii Your yacht will make no blip on anyone's radar – reflector or no reflector – and if it did, no-one would see it.

iv It is your life, and so it is your job to miss him, not vice-versa, because if he does hit you, he will probably never even know, and if he did, he probably wouldn't stop.

v No-one crosses the channel in a sailing yacht without being given a really deep-down fright at least twice.

There is one exception to this which I am proud to log – and that is the Royal Navy. The courtesy with which Frigates and Destroyers weave through clouds of Trog-boats is heartwarming and well worth the salute of dipping your ensign, which we should all be proud to do and which, incidentally, the Royal Navy almost always acknowledges.

On this general subject – the one thing every Trog Dad soon becomes an expert on is the wash of big steamers. Mostly he can see it coming because he's seen the big steamer and can tell everyone to watch out. It is never anything like as bad as that of the closely overtaking Gin Palace, but much depends on how much of the big steamer is under the water and the shape of her hull. Size isn't everything, and for example, the wash of the QE2 isn't much more than a quick rattle and then a gentle roll. The fast Cherbourg car ferries are another thing. They should be given a wide berth because there's a lot of lorry-weight inside them and they go pretty quick and make a wash like a young earthquake. As for the ferries – they don't disturb much water, but Dad learnt long since to give them a wide berth. They have their schedules to keep and know that if they jinked about for every one of the hundred yachts that'll get in their light each weekend trip, they'd never make it to Ryde, or Cowes, or Wooton, or Yarmouth, or wherever. The island ferries live like trams crossing Piccadilly circus, and they move, as the clerihew says, in pre-destined grooves, so better not argue the point.

But, in spite of all the hazards of dinghy races, minefields, Gin Palaces, ferries, hovercraft, QE2s and Esso Nells, a triumphant Dad finally makes it, through an X-class race, to Cowes Roads. His engine is still holding on, the ebb is still ebbing, and Mum, already having won her Marina point, is moving smoothly into the question of dining ashore.

9

Trog-Haven

As Dad chugs round for Cowes into the remnants of the wind and into the Medina estuary, he performs a couple of essential actions – he inclines a reverent head towards the Royal Yacht Squadron and he asks Mum to steer for a moment while he gets the sails down. It is the second of these which, he knows, will bring about the onset of another moment of truth, and one by which the rest of the weekend can be made or marred. Mum is very aware that the balcony of the Island Sailing Club is full of people with nothing else to look at for the moment but the sail taking down operation about to be deployed before them. She is also aware that there are large numbers of other boats milling about, including the Southampton Ferry coming up astern, and fears that every one of them will converge on her the moment they see she is left alone with the tiller. She equally believes that all this sail business should have been done at leisure and in privacy "out there" where there was bags of sea-room and no audience, and that Dad is a Trog-Positive for leaving it so late. Which he is. So Mum says "No". Either they go back into the Solent and do it there, or leave the sails up untii they are in the Marina, because there's no wind to bother them is there? Mum adds that divorces have been granted for less. Dad says not to be silly and it will only take a minute and Mum says that he heard what she said.

So, Dad compromises by nipping back among the moorings out in the channel and gets the sails down there, which could have been tricky if there had been any wind to speak of. This was, indeed, all Dad's fault. Had there been a wind he would have had to put the boat into it while there was still bags of room outside, and then Mum would have happily motored slowly to windward while he did his stuff on the deck and bundled the main up round the boom and tied it down. In light airs he didn't bother and was, properly, presented with an ultimatum.

On the occasions when there is an agile third hand sailing with Mum and Dad, these minor crises do not arise. Indeed, with an extra crew, all sorts of daring deeds may be attempted – like changing the foresail for a bigger (or smaller) one, poling it out, reefing or unreefing the main, or actually studying the chart and reading the pilot guide. Yet, sad to say, most of the family Trog cruisers just have a Mum and Dad on board.

I have often reckoned that an enterprising schoolmaster could fix up his male fifth and sixth formers with an all-found sailing trip every weekend by arrangement with the nearest yacht club. Lack of crew is a chronic complaint in the boats around our coasts and is, indeed, the limiting factor on the ambitions of many a Hornblower. A schoolmaster could also fix up his female sixth formers for weekends, but that might well all finish up in the News of the World.

Be all this as it may – a useful if meaningless phrase – Dad still has one job to do – actually getting a place in the Marina.

Until not so long ago there was no Marina at Cowes. Visiting yachts used to lie to pylons – which meant going alongside another boat, or small raft of boats, which were already tied up fore and aft to these wooden posts sticking up in rows out of the water. The drawback of this was that coming alongside was easy if there was someone on the other boat to take your lines, and not so easy if there wasn't. The trick was to select to lie by a boat which was inhabited and the counter-ploy was for its inhabitants to hide in the cabin and to leave their dinghy in a position of maximum obstruction to anyone trying to come up next door. In the end the visitor invariably finished, at the end of the day, with three or four boats both sides of him – all tied to the same pylons and all tied together with miles of breast-ropes and springs, and everyone with scores of fenders down.

It all used to be very matey and there tended to be lots of chat as between boat and boat, especially enjoyed by the Mums who compared wounds – moral and physical – and became united in a general aura of gin and mutiny. It was also good for the spoken French, as one of the boats was always from Cross-Channel.

A snag was that, dead on meal-time, the owner of the middle boat of the raft would return in his dinghy and say he was ever so sorry but he was leaving in ten minutes, but it should really be quite simple to get out without disturbing anyone very much. In such a situation there usually followed quite a splendid series of Trog happenings.

The prelude to all events, such as the one just envisaged, is that the various Dads appear in their cockpits and look wisely at all the ropes and at the offending boat and agree that it will be no real problem. They don't actually believe this for a second, and nor do the Mums who simply disappear. Any Trog progeny, however, pour out onto their appropriate foredecks because, like their soul-mates on the Broads, they have this built-in extra sensory perception for impending drama.

In the ensuing foreplay before action is joined, one of the Dads soon emerges as the leader of the enterprise and he now takes firm charge of the operation. He is, of course, by no means the best equipped to do so.

"If you go out this side," he pronounces to the candidate for departure, "then all we have to do is to take the stern warps from these three boats off the pylon – let you out astern – and then pull those boats back in again. It'll just be like backing out of a gate and then we'll swing the gate shut after you."

This plan is then adopted because none of the other Dads voices a better one, and those who belong to such of the boats as won't be directly involved are only too thankful to be spectators. The born leader, having set the strategy, then gives detailed tactical instructions to implement it. Soon the departing one has got no bits of string tying him to anything and is hanging on like grim death with hooks and hands, while the three boats on the outside swing out on their bow ropes – but with no other visible means of support. One of the other Dads does ask tentatively if they shouldn't have a warp ready to pass round the bows of the departing one so that the swinging part of the gate (three boats) can eventually be hauled back, because it's still ebbing isn't it? He wonders if they won't all go down-tide and end up the other side of the pylon and be right across and among the next-door raft of boats.

"Quite all right old boy," says the born leader, "all under control."

At this stage the departing one seizes his chance to dart out astern and motors clear of the carnage, waving farewells and saying, "Thank you all very much". He, in fact, is all right Jack, which is more than can be said for the born leader and his inshore squadron of three tied-together yachts which is now nicely across the tide and still swinging out. The hesitant Dad finally saves the day by throwing the warp he had quietly got ready, which the born leader grabs gratefully and is tugged back into line in the nick of time. "There you are," he says, "I told you it would be easy."

One of the best examples of the "letting out of the middle boat" which it has ever been my privilege to witness, was at Bembridge. The departing one, having been made way for, was due to hand over all the warps from the three outside boats to the waiting hands of the Dad of the inside boat. Instead, he just cast everything off, and the tied together raft of three went gloriously and fully adrift. At first those on board these three boats didn't actually realise what had happened and, by the time they did, it was too late. Shouts of rage speeded the departing one, and vain attempts were made to hook onto other moored boats, or to throw warps that were too short. The scene became very animated as Mums and children poured out to accuse the Dads of gross negligence and this resulted in three sets of purely domestic scuffles which became like plays within a play. Eventually, all three boats clanged heartily into the iron hull of a workboat at the down-tide end of the harbour and one crew fell into the mud.

A friend of mine and I watched this from our respective decks and, since we both knew the departed one very well indeed, we immediately adjourned to the club bar to concoct and embellish an authorised and revised version of the post-departure happenings so that we could tell him all about it – indeed, that very night. That's why he still thinks that one boat sank and two people had to be saved from drowning and I understand he has kept out of Bembridge ever since. He also believes the police are looking for him to help with their enquiries.

All this joy, as far as Cowes is concerned, was, as I said, in the good old days. There are still a few pylons for visiting boats, but the majority nowadays swallows three times and pays up for going into the Marina. I do not pretend to know the process by which much of the pylon area (which used to cost only a few bob as and when the Harbour Master collected it) has been enfolded into the private enterprise of the Marina, which costs a lot, lot more. The fact is that it has, and since it hasn't been "exposed" in Private Eye or on Nationwide, I assume it is all legal.

On the plus side, it must be said that Marinas provide a walk-ashore facility which cuts out dinghy work. But often, to get back and forth to the floating platforms which lead to the actual land, you have to clamber over two or three other boats which tend to be neutral about it – especially after midnight. There are, I agree, loos and showers and garbage disposal and water taps and, if you are determined enough, fuel. There are also hoses for washing down and, sometimes, electric sockets which, if you have a platform-side berth, you can plug into to charge your battery or to light the cabin, or both. That is if you carry a bulb and holder and a battery charger and a lot of wire lead, which, it so happens, I do.

Yet I am still unhappy about Marinas. Mainly, I think, because so many of them (here I am talking in general and not about Cowes) are so greedy. Long haired and un-affable young men, with all the loveable charm of a London traffic warden, stand aloof from such servile things as holding a warp for a moment, and wait impatiently while Dad works like a one-armed paper hanger to get tied up. Then they wave their little book in his face and say, "That will be two pounds" – or whatever. They are so palpably not there to help in any way, but only to collect cash that I find it irritating. The object of the exercise is just money and by no means service in return for money. There is also, on the face of it, not likely to be all that much bond of natural sympathy between students doing a holiday job and covered with revolutionary emblems, and anyone who has so ground down the faces of the starving poor as to be able to own a boat.

I much preferred the gnarled old hand whose contempt for the "yotties", while every bit as open as that of the fugitives from LSE and Essex, was not based on any political philosophy, but on the yotties' incompetence in a sphere in which he, himself, was highly efficient. It was, if you like, the honest contempt of the pro for the amateur – and the philosophy of it did not preclude giving a bit of help. Au contraire – because giving aid underlined the "competitive gap" as well as ensuring a tip. In short, it boiled down to pride of job which the LSE-ite "temporaries" don't have, and can't be expected to have – and, for my money, will probably never have – which sometimes, after a gin or two, makes me feel sorry for them.

Another thing about Marinas is the "extras". Some of them now charge for water and for use of the hose and, or so I have heard, for use of the loo. Maybe Cliff Michelmore, who comes from Cowes and belongs to the Cowes Corinthian along with Prince Charles, ought to examine one matter in his Holidays programme.

Which brings me to a very important subject. The Trog observer will notice that as soon as Dad has safely come into the Marina, and has cruised around waiting for someone to deign to tell him where to tie up, and has duly tied up, and has been moved again, and has paid his dues – then he and Mum will clutch their toilet bags and towels and make for the ablutions and the loos.

It is true that most boats have flushing toilets and some of them have them in compartments big enough for them to be used – but taps and main drainage have their own built-in charm, and there is a limit to the efficiency of battery driven razors.

There are, however, toilets and toilets, and the experienced non-Trog venturer and old campaigners will have them all logged for each harbour under the heading of "Essential Information".

At Cowes, for example, it is worth trying to join the splendid and not very expensive Island Sailing Club, if only for the facilities. There are many more good reasons for joining – like the bar and the balcony and the ability to eat there, and the right to fly an attractive burgee. But the showers and loos and the hot water are not to be sneezed at by any Dad or Mum. One of the joys of cruising, after a tiring series of beats from mainland to Island and back to get into Cowes, is to walk up from the facilities – freshly clean within and without, to take a drink out onto the balcony and enjoy the problems of all the other Trogs who haven't yet made it into the harbour. Truth to tell and, if it isn't sacrilege, Cowes itself is a pretty dreary place for ordinary yotties, being much over-hung with the glamour of the great international racing devices and the name-spangled jerseys of their crews. The whole place is one big "By Appointment" sign – even if some of them were to Queen Victoria – and all prices tend to match.

Way above Cowes and, indeed, above Folly Inn, and near the old Paddle-steamer-cum-restaurant-cum-bar, there is a Marina whose loos – at least when last seen – are really noteworthy. They are, in fact, proper little private dressing room and full toilet suites and are (or were) beautifully kept. Further, the Marina staff there actually appears pleased to see you and to lend a hand in getting you snug before the question of money is mentioned. By the time it is, one is very happy to pay.

One day I might even write a little "Loomanship" handbook on south coast harbours and their facilities, and on which clubs welcome visiting yotties and which don't. Club toilets and wash-eries are mainly very good – and some of them have little known back-doors which can be used when the front doors are firmly locked. In other harbours you have the choice between the public conveniences and knowing the right way up the staircases of the better hotels. Being clean and comfortable, and independent of the more limited facilities on board, is a matter which repays serious study, and the non-Trog will have made such a study. He will also carry in his toilet bag his own roll of loo paper. You never know what economics are being practised ashore.

There is one thing which can be said about life on board inside harbours or in marinas – it is seldom dull. In the first place, once safely in and snug, be it to pylons or to a platform, there is a great deal to look at. Those who are "in" are automatically in a position of superiority over those who are not. The ones that are still looking for somewhere to go, or are trying to squeeze into a small space by car-parking methods, or who are having problems generally, are on free show and they know it. The Trogs who are already safe, whose own boss shots at coming alongside are behind them, reckon they've paid their entrance fee by providing amusement for others, and now its their turn to be in the stalls. So, although the Dads and Mums are all ostensibly busy on board and going about their own business, what they are really doing is watching and hoping for someone else to have a disaster. Like getting stuck across a bowsprit.

Anyone who has ever had another boat's bowsprit jammed in its shrouds will wonder why Mr Desoutter ever invented the things. They are picturesque and Nelson had one, but they are a social menace and a weapon of war. Last season I saw a chap decide to leave a berth outside three Old Gaffers, all with ferocious bowsprits, and move into a vacant inside berth ahead of them. He planned to do it by pulling from the shore on ropes tied onto various parts of his boat.

After ten minutes he had his boat bows on to the berth and at right angles to the line of three bowsprits – each one of which was impaling some part of his rigging or his guard rails. I have frequently seen boats with one bowsprit stuck in them, but never had I seen three impalings at once and I took some photographs of it (which didn't come out). In the end, all the able bodied in the area had to help, and this had to be done on the principle of doing one of those pocket puzzles. It was no good clearing one bowsprit on its own, because the other two just got wedged the firmer. All

three had to be manoeuvred free at once, and then the victim had to be pushed sideways and clear in one gigantic heave. But as manoeuvrings which cleared bowsprit 'A' only further jammed bowsprit 'B', and put bowsprit 'C' through the cabin windows, it took a long, long time. At the end of it we got the other boat back to where it had come from, but all concerned had become a bit allergic to nostalgic chat about the picturesque and seamanlike origins of those pointed bits of wood.

And, if it isn't bowsprits, it's always something else – especially in the cool of the evening. This is the time when the harbour is full and its village occupants are getting mellow, and the room left for late-comers to manoeuvre is nil. Pity, then, the poor late-arriving Trog. No-one wants him alongside because this means more dirty ropes and more fenders and everyone has just tidied up and put on clean shirts. They have, in fact, retired behind a barricade of defensive rubber dinghies deployed in positions of maximum impedence, and the new boy is (quite falsely) told that there's bags of room "over there" – which means anywhere else except here. There is a visible atmosphere of non-collaboration and some of the established boats have notices on display which say, "Leaving at 4.00 am" – which would be the more credible if the faded writing wasn't clearly at least a season old. The ambience can be described as cool to discouraging.

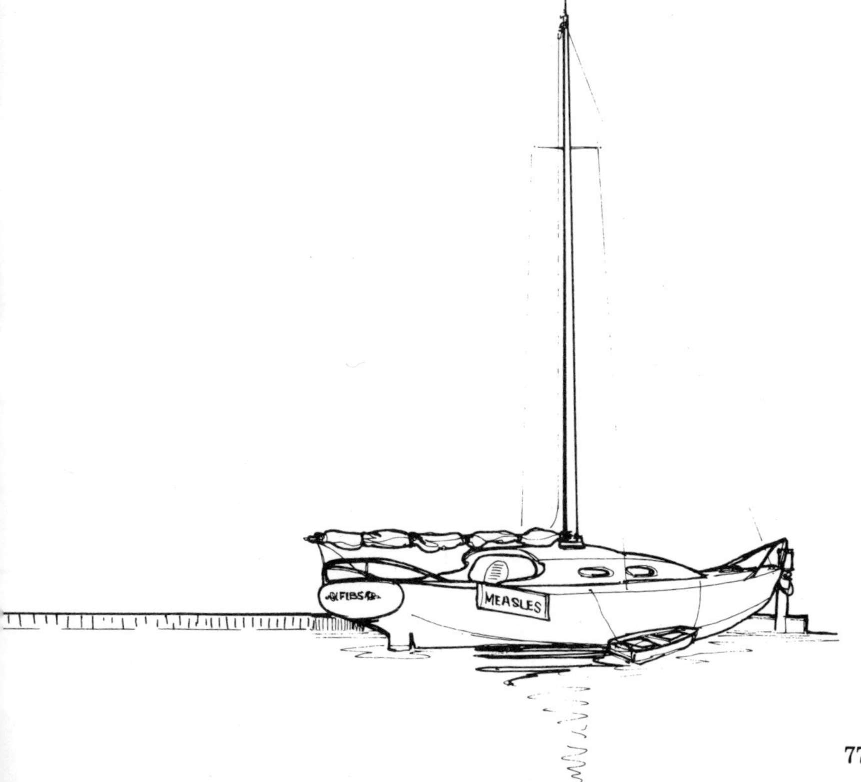

The counter ploy to all this is simply to ignore it and just to come alongside. It helps to pretend to be deaf or French or, better still, Dutch. I know someone who keeps a Dutch ensign just for such occasions, and he and his wife (who come from Dorking) have cultivated an attractive broken English in which they thank everyone profusely and invite one and all to visit their bulb farm on the canal at the back of Schipol. The British, of course, are always sympathetic to those who, through no actual fault of their own, are regrettably, foreigners. A French boat came alongside me several seasons ago and won our hearts by saying, "Can we come to you pliss and can you 'elp as we 'ave no bumpairs and no string". We still exchange Christmas cards.

Sunday morning is perhaps the best time for the Trog-observer to take his notebook down to his local Marina – somewhere about an hour before whatever is the change of tide for the day. The village will be divided into two clear and combatative halves: those who are catching the new tide stream and those who are not. The ones who are going are trying to extricate themselves, and the others are hauling on ropes and dragging boats about to facilitate their departure. In every corner of the visitors' area there is a real or potential happening. This usually features a boat which is trying to turn round in a restricted area and has got itself stuck, as it were, across the road, when other traffic is trying to use said road, and in both directions. So Mums and Dads will be pushing at the sharp ends and pulling at the blunt ends, and there will be no shortage of advice. If the boat has a bowsprit it will also, at some stage, be in someone else's shrouds. The Trog-observer – if he can tear his eyes and ears away – may also care to note that there are many boats which clearly intend to stay put in the Marina on account of they never do anything else.

Some may find it surprising that people will buy a boat and go to all the expense of Marina or mooring dues in order just to sit in it on fine weekends. I have to assure you that such is the case and especially is this so in river Marinas like those on the Thames. Such is the love of the Island Race for boats, and things to do with boats, that families will live aboard Friday night to Sunday night and never think of actually moving. Their vessels – often motor boats – are, in fact, floating weekend cottages from which they can fish and on which they can wear all the gear appropriate to rounding the Horn and have pictures taken.

There is a chap in one harbour I know – and you're not going to believe this – who picks up good money each weekend by nipping across on a ferry to a Marina and fetching over gin palaces and parking them in his local harbour. This is a giant journey of three or four miles. The owners then, themselves, come over on the ferry and occupy the gin palace for the weekend – wearing oilskins and the lot. On the Sunday nights they go home on the ferry and this chap takes their gin palaces back at leisure.

I have nothing against such Trogs – they are all good for trade – but as moorings and berths get ever more scarce, one wonders if they shouldn't be made to put their devices on the mud-flats. They would never notice the difference.

The time, however, has come for us to move on and out of the Solent – where Trog activity is spread over a dozen venues from Chichester to Yarmouth, and from Bembridge to Keyhaven – and to move to a place where every kind of known Trog action can be seen in the sweep of one coup d'oeil – Poole Harbour.

10

Poole Harbour

Just as all cats are four-footed animals while all four footed animals are observably not cats, it must be stated that all is not Trog that comes from Poole. Some of my best friends keep boats at Poole and I would be prepared to see any one of them marry my sister – if I had a sister – or my daughter, were she not already long wed to a scientist from Cambridge. Lack of prejudice can no further go than that.

I have singled out Poole Harbour for especial distinction merely because it is, so they say, the biggest expanse of harbour water in the world and, for ought I know, is in the Guinness Book of Records. And if you have a harbour as big as that, then there are going to be thousands of boats in it, and by the laws of nature, a large proportion of them are going to be very Trog indeed. As soon as you are on the approach to Poole you are left in no doubt on that score. Fleets of gin palaces and skimming dishes pour ceaselessly in and out at high speed, churning up the seas into mountains of wash, and playing 'last across the road' with the heavy commercial traffic which thumps remorselessly on. Where are you going to all you big steamers? Poole, Mate, and let the bloody yotties get out of our way.

Just around the corner from the Poole entrance – having dodged the chain ferry which goes across it – there is a major gin palace enclave, and there may be an empty mooring or two which you might be tempted to pick up for an hour or so of rest. A friend of a friend of mine did just this – having had a considerable all-night bashing on the way back from Cherbourg. Within five minutes a very snazzy launch was alongside and its boatman said, "You are not allowed to moor there. You must move on." To which this friend of a friend made a gruff two word nautical reply and went below again. To his surprise, the snazzy launch accepted his advice and just went away and the f. of a f. went back to sleep.

The question of picking up vacant moorings is, however, a vexed and vexing one. The general and civilised practise is that a visiting boat may pick up a vacant mooring temporarily, providing that the mooring is either obviously, or by clear statement of weight and size painted on it, man enough to hold the boat which is borrowing it. While on a borrowed mooring it is usually considered polite for the visitor to remain manned so that, should the owner return, the mooring can be immediately vacated in his favour. What is, therefore, very Trog indeed, is to hang onto someone else's mooring and shut the boat up while everyone goes ashore. The rightful owner cannot then use his own expensive mooring – nor dare he move the intruder, because he may well be liable for any damage, and nor can he "double up" onto the mooring, which may well break under the load. He is, in short, truly up the creek, and must either borrow another vacant buoy (if there is one) or anchor in what is almost certainly foul ground – or go some place else.

I write with feeling on this – someone having recently put his boat on my mooring and then gone off, in the event, for a fortnight. This kind of thing is a bit of a back-handed justification for Marinas, because if a Marina lets someone pinch your berth, it's up to them to shift the offender. Also, if you are bound for a visit to a Marina in another port, you can leave your dinghy back on your own mooring, which amounts to a public declaration of your intention to return in the pretty near future.

To be fair to Poole – once, when I was messing about looking for somewhere to anchor to ride out the strong ebb, a local boat, leaving its buoy, came over and said, "You can use my mooring if you like – I am going away for a week". I bless that chap, just as much as I once cursed the Poole gin palace that pinched my dinghy. (Why my dinghy was adrift in the Solent in a Force 5, gusting 6 – Westerly, is as long and inept a story as why I was towing it in rough seas in the first place.) But there it was, bobbing about, and I was beating hard to pick it up. I was about 200 yards away when this gin palace nipped in, hauled it aboard and made off with it – leaving me shaking my fist and scribbling down his name, rank and number, before calling it a day and ducking into Beaulieu. After a lot of telephoning that evening, I located the chap and he tried to bluff it out by claiming that there was no other boat within sight of him when he grabbed my dinghy and it was salvage wasn't it? So I said that if I wasn't there, how did I know the name and home harbour of his boat? So I got my dinghy back – albeit with a socking great puncture in it. He hadn't, of course, reported his "find" to the Harbour Master and, for all he knew, he might have been sitting on the evidence that somebody had been drowned. A real right Trog.

I have another grouse against Poole – and that is that the wash-battered quay wall, with quite a big rise and fall of water, has no built-in ladders – at least not where my yacht has ever got in. Nor has it any other amenity to justify a near Marina level of charges. Poole does, however, have a first rate new shopping centre in the town and a very good fish and chip shop. Chip shops – like loos – are logged by the older hands and given stars like hotels in the AA book and the Guide Michelin. They save Mum cooking an evening meal and save Dad paying several quid a head for dining out. Perhaps my little projected handbook should be called "Loos and Chips".

If, however, you keep away from the Custom House Quay and don't want any water (the hose doesn't reach very far) and are all right for fuel (which only comes "by telephoned appointment"), Poole is a beautiful Trog Haven. It has miles of scenic backwaters and creeks, and you can be shown the very spot of water in which Prince Charles landed in his parachute training drop. It is also great for fishing – and the fishing boats go out from the quay almost non-stop, laden with determined rod-bearing men and buckets full of dead mackerel as bait.

Trogs under training would be well advised to give all fishing boats a wide berth. They sit at anchor, usually over a "mark", which is in fact an uncharted wreck, and are surrounded by hundreds of yards-worth of lines which they get very angry if you sail into or over. They sit there all day, every weekend, tossing about, and they make one seasick just to look at them. The Solent boat fishers must have the most cast iron stomachs in the world. The other great fishing hazard is the lobster pot "field". There are a lot of these – like off Christchurch – hundreds of little black floating markers which you can hardly see and each one supporting tough bits of

string which can tangle round a motoring prop in a second. Once you have ever had a bit of warp – lobster pot or other – wrapped round your prop, you'll give all lobster pot minefields a wide, wide berth. There's no help for it but to put someone over the side with a knife – and if there's only Dad available – then bad luck Dad.

So – like I said – if you pick your spot in Poole and sit there quietly, you will have every kind of Trog-action paraded before you. You will see dinghies being capsized by gin palaces, and dinghies being capsized by their Dads. You will see innocents abroad in Mirror dinghies being scattered by the mass attacks of skimming dishes, and lots of yachts aground on the plentiful sandbanks which lurk on the edges of the many channels. Custom House Quay will also repay a studious visit. There you will find a collection of yachts – sail and power – huddled in rafts of three or four abreast, strung out along the wall. They will include a number of foreign boats and all will be being relentlessly and ceaselessly surged together, the combined inertia of each surge being expended by the inner boat of each raft against the wooden groynes with which the quay wall, at intervals, is faced. The cause of the surging will be the wash of the many and busy tugs and work-boats, perpetuated by the fact that there is another wall on the other side of the harbour which bounces back the wave of every wash as though it was a billiard ball rattling from cushion to cushion. There is little ambient happiness, but there are batteries of fenders, most of which have long since been squashed flat. The relative experience of the Dads of the inner boats can be judged by one simple test – have they got a bridging plank laid across the faces of the groynes, or are they trying to keep fenders out in station opposite each separate groyne? If the latter, they have no hope of maintaining the position, as each movement of the boat puts the fenders out of relative place, and is followed by the expensive noise of groyne crunching against unprotected boat. If they have got a plank out, then give them high marks, because they must have brought it with them – such things not being provided by the harbour authority.

Observe also, at low tide, if the inner Dad has managed to organise all the boarding ladders of the boats in his raft into one long ladder so that one and all can get up and down from the quay level, which is way above him. Hitching these ladders together calls for knotmanship of a high order, and I once saw one old lady take a very nasty tumble when the train of ladders parted. She did not, luckily, have to go to hospital – which was not the case with the poor chap who, plankless, was trying to replace fenders to match the groynes and got his hand in the way of an inward surge. I heard the crack of his broken bones from inside my cabin next door.

Also at the quay, the Trog observer can test out his gearmanship. There will be many holidaymakers on the parade and also many yotties. After a few minutes the student should be able to tell them apart at a glance, even though, superficially, they may be dressed much the same. The real yotties will, of course, eventually declare themselves by going on board, so the quiz results can be easily checked.

I suppose yottie identification works in somewhat the same way that I can pick out another Englishman clear across the width of Fifth Avenue, or in a beer cellar in Munich. And this is so, even if he is wearing, respectively, a Brooks Brothers suit or lederhosen; and I can't explain it by logic. I simply know. By the same token, once, when I was drinking wine at Koblenz before the war, and was only "visible" above the table to the extent of an open necked shirt which I had bought locally, a young German – a complete stranger – came to the table and carefully said "Abend" to everyone there, until he came to me, when he altered it to "Good Evening".

There is also no shortage of happenings at the quayside. The tide runs hard – so opening out a raft to let out an inside boat can be very fraught indeed – what with the tide and the workboat wash. There can also be crises with warps that were long enough when the tide was in, but are no longer so when the water level falls as far as it does. Your actual "dangling" situation, as earlier envisaged in a Thames lock, can really happen at Poole. Then there are the giant pleasure steamers whose berths are amid those of the yachts so that each steamer arrival and departure is a true test of nerves and of survival.

So, for all round study and enjoyment, I commend Poole Quay as being on a par with the bridge above Yarmouth – especially when there's an on-shore wind.

Finally

Anyone who reads our maritime history – and who doesn't? – cannot fail to be moved by the near miraculous way that the Island Race has always taken to the business of boats, even if they have never previously been nearer one than an office stool in Coventry.

In and around Nelson's day all sorts and conditions of men – gaol birds, unwary farm hands and the other casual victims of the press gang – found themselves crewing in ships in conditions of unbelievable privation. They had little to look forward to except the high chance of a terrible death, and if they survived, there was not all that prospect of their ever being paid. The discipline was that of a slave galley and they were often years without going ashore. Yet they became, not only the best seamen in the world, but the proudest. The poor devils even spontaneously cheered when told they were going to engage an enemy – this information being a virtual sentence of death for so many of them.

They were, on the face of it, the oppressed and downtrodden scum of the earth, yet,in battle after battle, their discipline and ability and pride of job saw inferior British forces beating the daylights out of Spanish and French and other European fleets whose coherence as a force rapidly dissolved under fire. The one time when the Royal Navy of the day got a bit of a run-around was from the American colonists, whose ships were also mainly commanded and manned by men from the same common stock.

Before I blunder on too far and find myself embarked on a thesis of a master-race, to which I do not, in fact, subscribe, I will content myself by repeating that we do have a perpetual national and natural love affair with boats. I also believe some of that emotion and ability has now been transferred to aviation, which has so much in common with the disciplines of the sea. The achievements and the spirit of the modern Royal Navy and of the Royal Flying Corps and the Royal Air Force, in two world wars, seem to me to have sprung from much the same roots, and certainly from much of the same tradition. Which is, perhaps, why the RAF Yacht Club has such a big membership and why so many of today's Admirals wear wings.

But, whatever the dark, or even primeval, reasons, the fact is that the Island Race uses up every bit of water it can find to float boats in. When I started to write this book, I had seen it, vaguely perhaps, as divisive as between Trogs and Non Trogs in all forms of water-borne devices. But the truth is that – with a few notable exceptions at national hero level – we are all Trogs of some kind.

There is not a man afloat, be it in a Mirror dinghy on a gravel pit, or in an ocean racer, who hasn't done something plain bloody stupid far more times than he will care to remember. Much more so than he would ever do in a car.

I have seen the bravest and best stuck in the silliest manner and I have been outsailed and out-manoeuvred by an old man in a cloth cap and braces who did it all one-handed because he was using the other to drink beer out of a sizeable stock of bottles.

Francis Chichester – that gentle and genuine Elizabethan, and who was an aviator before he turned yacht sailor ("It's the last outpost of true navigation"), once said to me, "When it really blows up in the Atlantic I can always go below and drink whisky till it stops. It's what you and all the rest of the weekend chaps do that really puts the fear of God into me. There you are – with mudbanks close on either side and hundreds of other boats and shipping all round, bashing about on lee-shores, often in a fog and with a lousy met forecast. I don't know how you do it." I, who regard Force 3 as a near gale and a visibility of two miles as a pea-souper, didn't actually personally deserve Francis's tribute, but so many other Trogs really do.

So, while we may find passing amusement in logging – as I have done here – some of our human frailties and pretensions, and while we may enjoy a slightly malicious laugh at someone else skidding on banana skins, let us not actually deceive ourselves. Whatever it is – except, perhaps, speed-washing other boats over – we've all done it and, what's more, we will almost certainly do it again.

Whenever I am too openly enjoying someone else's mooring-up troubles – my wife reminds me of the time when I tried to go alongside a raft of boats down-tide and eventually had to be towed out of the resulting mess by a passing motor launch. Or the time, scrambling on board in the dead of night in the Hamble, when I said, "all right, pass me the dinghy painter", only to be told, "but I just gave it to you". (We got the dinghy back the next day). I recall also that a vastly experienced chum got pinned broadside on to Yarmouth pier by the spring flood – and it took (as I tell the story) the Yarmouth lifeboat and the Lymington ferry to drag him out of it.

Even the most glamorous Admiral's Cup type racers, with resounding names on board, can get their spinnaker in a real Giles-like robble, as I once had great pleasure in observing just off the Nab. Now I have never ever had a spinnaker in a robble. I don't own a spinnaker and, if I did, I would never ever be allowed to try to hoist it. I did mention the subject once, but the crew made it unambiguously clear that this was mutiny material and should never be raised again. Incidentally, I once saw one of our most famous W.W.2 Generals with his spinnaker wrapped, not once, not twice, but five times round his forestay and he was still visible, sorting it out over an hour later.

So, Trogs we all are and the great thing is that we should know it and enjoy it. It is even possible, just now and then, that the Mums enjoy it too – maybe on a lovely calm evening in a picture postcard harbour, and when the wine is good and the company merry, and the men have done the cooking, and the swans glide by, and the boat next door has got its anchor beautifully fouled and its dinghy painter round its prop. Then – for a magic moment – all is of the best in the best of all possible worlds.

P.S.
Since finishing this book it has been pointed out that I have failed to enlarge on the snobbery and Troggery of flying or 'wearing' ensigns, burgees, and assorted other flags.

I can only say that all that has ever been written about Old School Ties, fades pale before the one-upmanship afloat of club burgees and ensigns.

The superior sneer of the helmsman of a Blue Ensign boat (meaning roughly there's an 'R' in his club) as he encounters a run-of-the-mill Red Ensign is only surpassed by the aloof superiority with which the White Ensign of The Squadron passes all.

The only face-saving question an out-ensigned or out-burgee-d Trog can ask - and he can only ask it of himself - is 'is he entitled to it?'

He will never know.

Meanwhile, my favourite character of the season is the chap who attracted a Rescue helicopter and a lifeboat by flying, at his cross-trees, a flag for 'I require immediate medical assistance' and who later said 'I put it up because it looked so pretty'.